Diary

of a

Missionary Nurse

Patrecia Gray

True Potential
REACH THE WORLD

All Scripture quotations, unless otherwise noted, are from the King James Version of the Bible.

Diary of a Missionary Nurse

Cover and Interior Page design by True Potential, Inc.

ISBN: (Paperback): 9781960024756

ISBN: (e-book): 9781960024763

LCCN: 92025913314

True Potential

True Potential, Inc.
PO Box 904, Travelers Rest, SC 29690
www.truepotentialmedia.com
Cover and Interior Page design by True Potential, Inc.

IN NEW GUINEA — Rev. and Mrs. Lawrence Gray, Robin and Mendy, left recently for Papua, New Guinea, to do missionary work. Rev. Gray was the pastor of the Gospel Tabernacle on Viand Street before leaving for New Guinea.

Gray Family In New Guinea As Missionaries

"We may have different religions, different languages, different colored skin, but we all belong to one human race."[1]

There are more than 10,000 different ethnic groups in the world and every one of them is unique and deserves equal respect and recognition. Due to rapid globalization, the destruction of traditional environments, and conflicts on racial and religious grounds, many ethnic minorities are on the verge of total extinction. Their rich ancestral knowledge, traditions, and languages are rapidly disappearing. It is important to tell the world about these unique people and their ancient cultures, to share their wisdom, show their faces, and tell their stories as members of our human family.

---

1   Kofi Annan, Secretary-General of the United Nations between 1997 and 2006

Contents

Preface

The content of this book comes from my diaries, which hold my memory captive with paratexts of memories that deliver the following stories with many happenings—the delightful, the destructive, and the miracles.

Papua New Guinea is an island where palm trees sway and the moon seems so close you could reach out and touch it. The spray from the beautiful bluish-green Pacific waters laps the shores. Sweet pineapples and orange papayas grow as big as footballs. Luscious guava trees and banana plants wait for the kids to come get their snacks. Lemon trees are so loaded with fruit their branches have to be supported.

In between all the vexations, there are the wonders of the island's green verdure, the bright red poinsettias that grow freely by merely sticking one end of their stems into the ground, where grow roses and thorns, beauty and ashes, satisfaction and suffering, and where for eight years Diary of a Missionary Nurse boarded a flight.

Papua New Guinea, PNG, is a totally unique habitation of its own.

PNG claimed its official independence from Australia's control on September 16, 1976, even though Australia's influence still permeates the atmosphere. Up until this time, many people labeled it as the "stone age."

After twelve years of preparation to go to the land of tall mountains, tropical rain forests, and big snakes, we arrived in PNG in February of 1977.

The island has its own particular scent like nothing else to compare it to. The land is rich in oil, gold, cacao trees, coffee trees, timber, and copra.

The people are friendly, strong, and helpful. PNG, like other countries, has its "rascals" as they are called, who can steal, kill, and destroy; yet you can stand on the sidelines as they are in battle with another tribe and they will not willfully harm you.

Some people, when they heard we were going to Papua New Guinea, asked, "Where is that? Is that in Africa?"

Then we explained, "No, it's not Africa. It is, at the nearest point, as one source claims, one hundred miles north of Australia."

To describe Papua New Guinea in its entirety would take a book within itself. As for me, it is loveable, and it is unique.

Names in this book may have been changed for privacy

Introduction

Twelve Midnight at Point Pleasant, West Virginia

The year was 1960, inside a big yellow house with a mint green living room, a cold fireplace, and Grandpa in bed in the next room. People sat waiting for the clock to strike midnight. A Christmas tree stood in the corner with small glowing lights that twinkled and tinsel that glimmered. A robust woman, whom they called Grandma, sat next to the bright shimmering Christmas tree, with her teenage daughter, Aunt Barbara, across the room in a straight chair.

An eighteen-year-old boy, Lawrence Gray, better known as Larry, wandered about the room.

Over on the left side of the room, on the couch, sat my parents quietly waiting with their teenage daughter, that's me, Patrecia.

I felt thirsty as the hands on the clock drew closer to twelve o'clock. I asked, "Can I have a drink?"

Grandma said, "Barbara take her to the kitchen and get her a drink." I followed her to the yellow kitchen, where she got a glass from the cabinet, turned on the spigot, and gave me a glass of tepid water to drink. "Yuk!" I sipped slowly as I waited. The water scarcely quenched my thirst.

I had only a few minutes left, as I had previously known time. A medley of concerns raced through my mind—do I, or do I not; if I do, I will never be my own person again. The clock gave its summons twelve times.

The reason of youth propelled me back into the living room where the scant party waited for whom the bells toll…12:02 a.m.

Larry and I walked together and stood beside the cold dark fireplace and in front of the Christmas tree with its beautiful blue, red, green, and yellow lights shining brightly.

Grandma, a licensed minister, stood before the lighted Christmas tree with Larry and me. She began with the wedding vows, "We are gathered here…" and ended with, "Lawrence, do you take this woman to be your lawful wedded wife?"

He said, "I do."

She then asked, "Patrecia, do you take this man to be your lawful wedded husband?"

I said, "I do."

Grandma then said, "I pronounce you man and wife."

That was pretty much the end of it – no cake and no refreshments – only the tepid water I drank before.

When two people say, "I do" in marriage, it is like signing your name to a blank check. Little did either of us know those "I dos" would lead us to the other side of the world, to the island of Papua New Guinea. Neither of us, Mr. and Mrs. Lawrence Gray, knew "it would be like this."

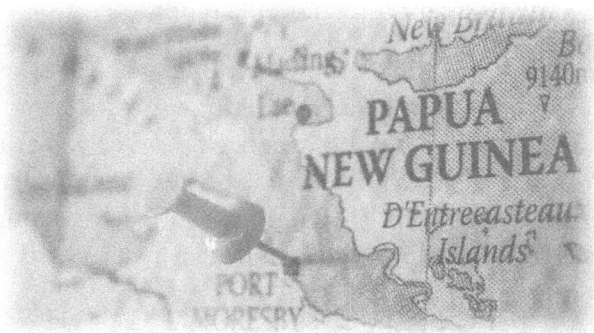

1: A Broken Vow

The place was Kaupena Mission Station in the Southern Highland Province of Papua New Guinea.

"Thursday morning, Togapa broke his vow to God. Thursday evening, on his way to Illiabu on his motorcycle, a big truck came around the bend and ran into him. Now he's out there...dead."

Chants came rolling down, through the trees, over the clouds, and up the mountains, while daylight rubbed its eyes. The earth shook as the tribes stomped in unison, twirling their axes, spears, and brandishing their bows and arrows. As a new missionary, I thought, *this is like a parade, or are we standing on the threshold of death? The brisk air of the morning awakened my senses; this is for real. Will our names be entered into a book of martyrs?*

A little boy named Togapa lived with his dad in the Tona area, and then his papa bought ground at Kaupena and moved his family there. Togapa grew up, went to school, and became a government teacher. To be educated in the Highlands of Papua New Guinea was a coveted sign of prestige and position, so both the Tona Tribe and the Kaupena Tribe claimed Togapa for their own, which could mean tribal trouble.

I was standing in the kitchen by our wood cook stove when there was a knock on our back door. A station helper came asking for Mr. Gray.

He said, "Togapa was going around a bend on his motorcycle up toward Iliabu when a big truck hit him and killed him."

Larry got the message and took our station's gray Toyota truck to pick up the body. Before he got back, a government truck came pulling onto the station with Togapa's body in the back. The driver drove across the airstrip up to the closed clinic and laid the body on the veranda. People began to gather, wailing and mourning with tears running down their reddened cheeks. Togapa's friends rubbed over him as if to bring him back to life, but he was dead.

I went up to the clinic to where the body lay and wondered, *why and how this could happen. The evening sky is graying. It's misty and dismal. There is such a strong feeling of judgment that it seems to penetrate throughout the mountains. The feeling is so intense that it feels like a knife could slice through it. Why is all of this dying? Why?*

This month, death seems to float over the mountain like vapor from dry ice.

This morning another little boy was brought to lie on the mission station…dead. This month, death seems to float over the mountain like vapor from dry ice. Wailing…wailing, we hear it night and day, people crying and wailing for the dead. All of these deaths, at one period of time like this, are unusual and eerie.

Everywhere we go, even inside our house, we still hear people crying and wailing for the dead. It feels like a dying plague.

We are told the people who cry will be given a feast afterward. Please, no disrespect, but they should not be hungry when it stops.

People are still coming in to mourn over Togapa's body. The tribal brothers' emotions are welling up between sadness and anger at the successful contender. Someone alerted the police, and the police came to take the body away for an autopsy. His people didn't want the body to leave them; they powerfully didn't want it to go.

Glaimi, another little boy of the village who had grown to a government position, talked to them, so they let the police take Togapa's body. Now all they had was talk and their angry emotions. They began talking about fighting the tribe of the man who took Togapa's life.

The next day, Sunday, Mac Arthurs, a missionary couple from the Australian sawmill camp down the mountain, came up to church, and then over to our house for dinner.

At 11 a.m. we heard chants coming down the mountain from above our house. Then we heard a second group of warriors chanting behind the first group. Both groups crossed through the mission station and down the mountain to the main graveled highway.

Men from one of the tribes came asking if they could bury the body on the mission grounds, but there was concern that would cause more trouble if they did, so Larry, my husband, and Kepalaya, the station's head pastor, went to Pabarabuk to talk to Brother Glick, the field superintendent, about the situation.

A report came in that seven tribes have gathered about a half-mile down the mountain at the main road, and they are causing trouble. The reporter said they attacked one man's truck. Glaimi, the government official, tried to stop them, but they wouldn't listen to him. The police heard about the ruckus and came and set off tear gas. Beverly Wickham, the other missionary nurse, was trying to get back up the mountain to the mission when she was overcome by the tear gas. She said, "My chest felt like it was crushing, and I was nauseous."

Five days later, again people came to gather over Togapa's unembalmed body. They had put the body inside a box and put the box inside the closed clinic. They wanted to hang the box up on poles, like their old custom, but Larry told them they couldn't do that on the mission station.

A few years earlier, when a good PNG man died, the men would put the dead body up in the air on poles, on a flat surface in the sun. Then some of the boys and men would sit on the ground beneath the decaying body and let the decaying body juices run down onto them. They said they believed this would make them strong and integrate the spirit of the dead with theirs.

Togapa's tribal brothers were going to take his body down to the road *bung* where people gather. Another tribe said, "No. Leave it here at the station."

It wasn't long until we heard war chants coming up the road toward the station. I went out to the side of the airstrip, where the road intersects with the station, to see what was happening. There they came; lines and tribes dressed in war garb; paint, feathers, and barely clad bodies, marching up the road approaching the station.

Self-Imposed Army

The sound came closer until I could have reached out and touched their pig-greased bodies that were covered with bright red and yellow colored warrior paint...but I did not dare. More tribal warriors marched, uninvited, onto the mission station to stake their claim from another tribe... for a schoolteacher's body that they claimed as one of their tribe.

A messenger said to me, *"Meri bilong Togapa, em i karim pikini long et pela mun. Na ol I bugarapim long taim em I stap wantaim long ol man na meri."* I was new to this Pidgin "trade talk." It was put together in different languages for trade purposes, but with help, I figured out what he said. He said the wife of Togapa, the man whose corpse lay out on the airstrip, was eight months pregnant, and she had been hurt. He said, "The tribes started fighting while she was kneeling beside Togapa's body. They took her to Beverly's house. They want you to come."

I set out to get to the other side of the busy road through a space between the marching tribes. Over in Beverly's house, Nancy, Togapa's wife, lay on a board couch. After assessing her condition, I knelt beside her while she told this painful story—how and why Togapa was dead.

She said, "On Tuesday, Togapa seriously prayed and told the Lord he was miserable, and that he wanted to live for Him. He promised he would quit smoking and drinking, and straighten up his life, but if he went back on his promise to The Lord this time, He could take his soul to the place of fire."

She said, "I told Togapa to go to prayer meeting Wednesday night and publicly give witness to this. Wednesday night came, and so did one of his friends. He didn't go to the prayer meeting that night. The next morning, Togapa broke his vow to God and he started smoking."

She said, "Thursday evening, he was on his way to Iliabu, you know, that little town up the road. He was on his motorcycle when a big truck came around the bend and ran into him. Now he's out there…dead."

Nancy said, "I wanted to know where he went, so I asked God for a sign. If he went to heaven, let a sign happen to his fingers. If he went to the place of fire, let a sign happen to his face."

She said, "As I knelt beside him, white stuff came out of his nose."

She continued, "Two tribes claim him as one of theirs because he was educated and an educated member of the tribe represents a great honor for the tribe, and that's why they are fighting. They knocked me over, and they said they put a curse on my baby."

They knocked me over, and they said they put a curse on my baby.

Those of us with Nancy prayed that God would intervene, help Nancy, and give us a miracle—to stop the fighting. After a short while, Nancy seemed stable, so I left.

I walked out the front door toward the airstrip, and what I saw was nothing short of amazing! Those same fighting enemies, who were in a tribal war just moments ago, were sitting around on the ground listening to Larry, as he stood tall, 6'2" in the middle of them preaching—about the "peace" of the Kingdom of God.

How those tribal warriors stopped fighting, went down to the *matmat* cemetery to bury Togapa's body, then came back, sat down as one, and listened to Larry preach about the peace of the kingdom of God is still a miracle remembered to this day.

The series of judgments of deaths seemed to have stopped with Togapa.

It was a Sunday, a few months after Nancy's baby was born; we looked out our window and saw her standing. She brought the baby to our door with the curse still on it.

15

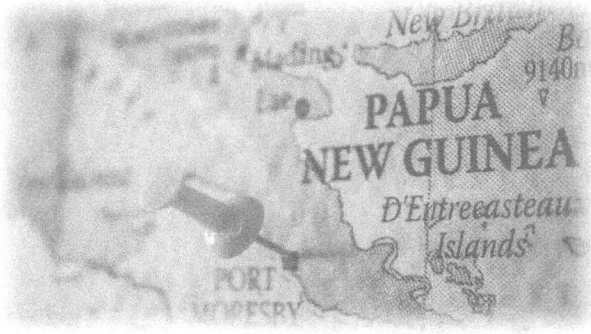

2: The Curse on Baby Togapa

October 14, 1977

I cooked almost all day for tonight's guest. This morning while I was fixing breakfast, a girl came to our door and said, "Nancy is at Beverly's house. She delivered her baby, will you come?"

I left the steaming gravy on the table and the hot biscuits in the warm oven and went over to Beverly's house. Nancy and the baby appeared to be doing fine...

Later, I went to Beverly's house to decorate Robin's cake for tomorrow. Robin is my soon-to-be sixteen-year-old daughter, and we are planning a few surprises for her.

I got home late in the evening and was very tired. Dishes were not washed, no fire was in the wood cook stove, and there was no dry wood to put in the stove.

"Where there is no wood the fire goes out." Proverbs 26:20
The evening went into the night when Larry came in and announced, "We need a place for twenty people to sleep. They had vehicle trouble and it is too dangerous here for them to be out at night." He also said, "They need something to eat, can we fix rice for them?" "We," meaning, "you."

Kyiaksi, our garden boy, brought in wet wood. I proceeded to get out my largest heating pail, but first, I HAD to lie down and rest.

Our wood cook stove

Robin finished preparing the supper. After that, Larry tried to show slides on the 16 mm projector, but neither did it work.

Sunday 16

Today is Robin's birthday. Larry is off to an outstation for Lotu church this morning. About 3:00 p.m., we had a small party for Robin with other missionaries and a few visiting workers from the Australian mission down over the mountain.

4:30 p.m.: Nancy Aiye, Togapa's widow, stood outside at our door. We invited her in. She brought her new baby for Beverly to look at.

Nancy said, "The baby cried last night, and today she would not eat."

I had worked in labor, delivery, and the nursery in the States, so I took the little bundle in my arms. She stopped crying. I wondered at first about colic until I felt slight jerking movements.

Nancy took the baby in her arms; it began to cry again and turn cyanotic. She told us this is what it had been doing.

Beverly thought it might be the beginning symptoms of neonatal tetanus, which is common in PNG. Some women use pieces of regular bamboo or other unsanitary sharp objects to cut the umbilical cord.

We debated, what should we do? Going to Mt. Hagen where there's a doctor is a big deal and it takes preplanning.

Larry said, "We could take them to Mt. Hagen to the doctor, then stay until morning and pick up a ton of rice for the mission store." We quickly prepared; Robin would stay with Beverly, and Mendy, our youngest daughter, would go with us.

The mother, baby, Larry, and I managed to get into the cab of the station's gray Toyota truck while Mendy and the usual crowd that always wants a ride to somewhere got onto the back.

A few miles down the bumpy gravel road, the baby began to cry again and again began to turn cyanotic. I took her onto my lap and started the two-finger heart compressions on her little chest. We prayed and she calmed again. This was repeated a couple more times before we reached the hospital.

When we arrived at Mt. Hagen, we went straight to the receiving building of the block hospital where a few chairs were set against the wall. It was one of PNG's prestigious third-world hospitals.

A young man, *"sister"* as they call their Registered Nurses, sat inside the receiving ward. He nonchalantly told us to have a seat. The baby began to cry, and again she stopped breathing. Immediately, I started the heart massage and called to the male nurse, "You better come!"

He came over, grabbed the baby, and took off running for help — outdoors. He ran over to another building looking in room to room for help. Then he went running down the hall and into a nursing ward where he found oxygen and a suction machine. Upon hearing the commotion, several medical people came to help with the little, fatherless, few-day-old baby. Work as they might; the baby's heart stopped. It quit!

I went to be with the young mother whose tears rolled down her face. She not only agonized as a widow but now as a mother bereaved of her only child.

Later, Dr. Bevis, the Australian doctor, came in to check the little bundle. He said he thought it could have been meningitis or septicemia. He said we could take the body home tonight, or leave it so they could do an autopsy to find out for sure the cause of death. Maybe out of curiosity, we stayed.

Larry and I found a room at Mapang, a house for missionaries for when they come to town. They had a room that had not yet been cleaned, with a small bed where the previous national occupants had just left. Nancy lodged over at the hospital.

The Sting of Death

Larry went to get cargo, while I visited another missionary who was in town trying to recover from Amebic Dysentery.

Larry and I then went to get Nancy and her infant's corpse. The doctor's report gave the reason for death as "pneumonia" and then said, "The inside of this baby was a mess."

This precious baby was alive inside her mother until its own tribal people fought over the body of this child's father and claimed to have laid a curse on his offspring.

Was it really the curse? One thing we know for sure is how destructive and powerfully shattering "sin" is, which the Bible tells us is the "sting of death."

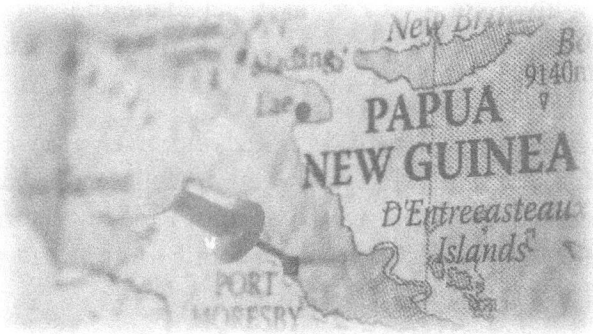

3: Leaving the Womb of America

February 16, 1977

The weather is cool here this morning in Summerfield, Florida, but the excitement is high. We are getting ready to leave for the other side of the world. I wondered; *am I dreaming?* No, because I hardly slept during the night.

It feels unreal that after twelve years of studies and preparation, my family of four is leaving the womb of America and going to the land of our calling as missionaries to Papua New Guinea, the Big Island in the South Pacific.

It is now 4:00 a.m., and we are packing our last-minute necessities and getting ready to leave our blessed homeland of plenty, for a third-world country once known as the Stone Age.

"We have to pull out of here for the Orlando airport by 5:00 a.m.," said Larry.

We stuffed our bare essentials into our limited suitcases, and the scales read – too heavy. It is repack – once more; and once more try again. There we have it, nearly nothing to stay within our allowed weight per person for the airline for the next few years in a far-off country where Malaria is endemic and snakes are big enough to eat a small child.

One missionary told us as he was driving on his way home up in the Highlands of PNG, he saw a Python stretched out in front of him all the way across the graveled Highlands Road. That, I am not looking forward to. I care little for snakes.

Now for the countdown; we have stored and given away our seventeen years of married collectibles, and have hopefully procured the necessities we need for our future years. We eliminated and eliminated again until our suitcases and footlocker for a family of four had reached their 55-pound limit—for each.

I looked around, checking in corners, and in all of the rooms for anything we may have left behind in the small two-room guesthouse at our mission's headquarters in Summerfield, Florida.

Larry was finishing fortifying our luggage when I asked, "Where is it? Where is my concise *Matthew Henry Commentary* that dad just bought me?"

"Sorry, we can't get it in," Larry said.

"I'll ask Lillian (my sister-in-law) to mail it to me." I never saw it again. That wasn't the only thing I would never see again.

Mom and Dad came to Florida from Ohio to spend the last few days with us at the mission headquarters before our departure.

Mom said, "I don't think my heart can stand watching you step onto that plane." They left last night.

This morning, before closing the door to the mission's guest cottage, I looked around to where Mother and Dad had been. The smell of savory roast and sweet caramel popcorn still lingered in the air that we had fixed together before they left.

A car awaited us outside. My husband, two daughters, and I walked out into the dark and climbed into the waiting car. The shadows left me with ill-defined memories of Mom and Dad, while gray clouds draped their arms around me as thoughts of leaving my known world behind masqueraded in my head.

We nestled into the veering vehicle
It was like a thousand years
and a million midnights
of remembrance.
While en route to the airport,
"Mom…Dad!"
I could feel the pain
of another slice
on the umbilical cord
as it was being severed
as we were leaving the womb of America.
Would we ever see each other again?
The mission's director and his wife,
Larry, our two daughters, and I
Journeyed on down the road.
I sat in the back seat alone,
Yet, not alone, but
Shrouded by obscurity,
Leaving all I ever knew.
I then heard the
The mission director's wife,
Sitting next to me
Humorously say,
"One mature missionary,
as he was leaving
his American homeland said,
'I want my momma!'"

We finally arrived at the Orlando, Florida airport for more unfamiliar experiences.

Am I Dying?

This new life feels strange. My two daughters and I had never been on a plane or even in an airport before. We were to learn how important strict airline time and schedules are.

We got in the line-up that corralled us out onto the tarmac. We climbed the steps into the upper belly of the plane and into our assigned seats.

I feel the curved walls and ceilings closing in on me. I feel like I am inside of one of those old gray, elongated Electrolux sweepers…air dried and vacuum packed. Is this what it's like to be inside a vacuum sweeper? I kept taking deep breaths that were hard to get.

The plane is slowly moving. Now it's turning. Why is it stopping? I have the ability to panic. It's like I could hear my Dad's voice in the walls, "You can do it; you can do it." I had to do it for my husband and girls' sake, for my sake, and for God's sake.

It was 9:00 a.m.—lift-off time. Little by little, I became acclimated to my environment, but the change in air pressure caused our daughter's ears to pain. I tried finding chewing gum in my purse. Robin was feeling nauseous. The plane provided a complementary paper bag in the seatback; she held it in her hands—just in case. Comforting my daughters afforded me less time to take thought of myself.

The plane ride smoothed out and so did we… "Oh look, there's the 'grandiose' Grand Canyon," I told the girls, "It's unmistakably breathtaking."

We arrived in San Francisco at 12:05 p.m. (3:05 p.m. eastern standard time (EST)). I called Mom and Dad to hear their voices one more time before leaving earth, uh, America.

Again, we took to the air. Our next touchdown was in Seattle, Washington, and then we landed at Vancouver, Canada at 5:30 p.m., where we overnighted at the Airport Inn.

At 3:00 a.m. I woke up with my heart pounding rapidly and a weird sensation, as if I could die. "Larry, are you awake? Please wake up and pray for me."

He prayed, "Lord what do I do? My wife is sick and we are on our way off of this continent, far away from home to a land where we've never been and know little about. Do we go to the hospital; do we go back, or do we go onward? Amen." His faith was being tried

> "Lord what do I do? My wife is sick and we are on our way off of this continent..."

as if by fire. After he prayed, he felt a peace, "It's okay. We'll go on."

We can't turn back, we just can't. We both had graduated from Universities; and prepared our lives for twelve years around this trip, and now we are on our way to Papua New Guinea as missionaries to fulfill our dreams, plans, and calling.

I always carry baby food in my purse for when my blood sugar gets too low, which is called hypoglycemia. Something similar happened several years before at the amusement park in Huntington, West Virginia. We were attending the Evans Super Market picnic, which was the company Larry worked for. I had not eaten and it was noon. I stood in the long, slow line for lunch when I felt like things were spinning around.

"Larry, I have to sit down."

He took me over to a table and set me down until he could get me something to eat. Now, here we are in Canada getting ready to leave the North American Continent, and my hand is shaking.

"Larry, please hand me the little jar of baby food in my purse." I ate a little, but there wasn't much of a change. "If I can just get up and let the water run over me in the shower, maybe I could feel better."

Larry helped me into the shower room.

Ooh, that warm water feels so good. It is baptizing my ill body. It did help a little, but things still didn't register. I know I am here, but I'm not. My heart has settled down a little, but not to normal.

Sleep was finished for the family. We packed up and carried our luggage toward the lobby.

"Larry, please, can you get me some bread? I'm still feeling faint." He came back with two slices of toast. I tried eating one, but it too didn't help.

Through it all, I vaguely remember a waiting room with people in it. I looked around, continuing to feel like a stranger in my body.

While still ill at 8:00 a.m., we boarded the Canadian Pacific Airlines (CP Air) headed for Honolulu. The stewardess guided us to our separate seats. She seated me next to the window. The woman beside me said something about being the pilot's wife. Still lethargic, I took little notice of reality.

Once we were in the air and leveled off, the stewardess brought breakfast and set it on our pull-down trays from the back of the seat in front of us. "Sausage links and bacon" is what I remember. I put that protein in my mouth and savored that flavor. All right! It was like someone turned on the lights. I came home. Protein! Now, my surroundings made sense; we were headed for Honolulu, and thank God after a little while, things were right again. Thank God for that ram (pork) He provided in the thickets.

The ram in the thickets refers to the Bible's Old Testament where Abraham showed his obedience to God by offering his only true son as a sacrifice. However, when Abraham raised the knife to slay his son, God placed a ram over in the thickets, to offer instead of his son. This was an example of how God would, in time, offer His only begotten Son. This was also a test of Abraham's faith and obedience to God. He passed with flying colors. Jehovah Jireh equals God provides.

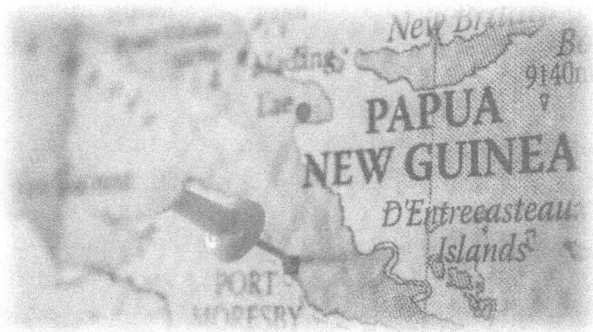

4: "Liqueurs Anyone, Liqueurs?"

February 1977

It is now Friday instead of Thursday. We became one day older in a moment of time. We have flown for miles, miles, and more miles over the blue, expansive Pacific waters while crossing the International Date Line. Daylight, daylight - noon looks like it's been hanging around for a long time.

Dehydration sets in when flying long distances, and my mouth is so dry. I am forever asking for a drink of water. One Qantas Airlines male steward told me, "Every time I see you, I think of water." I thought, *that works both ways*.

We are now on our way to Nadi International Fiji Airport. We are in mid-air, and an elderly man is talking excessively loud, and he's becoming unmanageable. The folk in this aircraft are becoming uneasy with concern.

For air miles, the attendants have been repeatedly asking, "Liqueurs anyone, liqueurs?" Is it any wonder the poor old fellow is looped? He is quarrelsome and disorderly. The more he drinks, the more disruptive and unpredictable he becomes. The flight attendant who served him his drinks is now trying to console him.

I am glad to be landing at Nandi, Fiji to get my feet back on the ground. Larry and Robin stayed on the plane while Mendy and I got off to walk around for the half-hour touchdown to say, we had put our feet on Fiji soil.

Lo and behold, inside the airport, there goes that old man making his way to the bar for another drink…guess he is thirsty.

"All aboard" toward Sydney. We're back in flight, and not one of those previous, tense moments changed the beauty of Fiji's luscious green patchwork fields. Fiji is our first touch of real tropics; it's utterly intriguing.

Each flying mile brings us closer to our destination. We have one more stopover and that is Sydney, Australia.

The voice on the intercom just said, "We are in a severe storm. The Sydney airport is closed."

The voice on the intercom just said, "We are in a severe storm. The Sydney airport is closed. We may have to go to Brisbane to land."

I believe the pilot because our plane is going up and down like a bucking bronco. We await our fate. Robin is ill. She is complaining of her ears hurting. She has the "emesis" bag from behind the seat in front of her, just in case. The passengers are restless but frightfully quiet. There is an eerie feeling enveloping inside this capsule. Will we live or will we die? *If we live or die, I never want to repeat this again.*

After a twenty-year, uh—twenty-minute turbulent storm we finally reached the beautiful shimmering turf of the Sydney runway. It feels so good to be on the ground again. Whew! Now I can say, it was a good landing anyway you put it—*Jehovah Jireh* equals *God delivers*. He provides the ram in the thickets.

After we got through customs, we then checked in our baggage. We were quite a spectacle going through customs dragging our luggage with cameras and radios hanging on to whatever body parts would carry them—into a strange place – on the other side of the world.

We're definitely not sure if, where, how, or what we are supposed to do. I guess you can say we are broadening our portfolio of experiences.

At last, we managed to get an airport bus to take us to the Crest Hotel at 12:05 a.m. Australian time, which is 15 hours ahead of the folks back home and our body's "cicada" clock.

Wow! What is this thing hanging up on the wall behind the commode? Oh, it's a commode tank.

I suspect this is the beginning of the first things we will wonder about.

Up again at four and back on a Qantas plane at 8:00 a.m. At twelve o'clock, someone cried out, "It's over there," speaking of the beautiful, impressive, green island of Papua New Guinea.

The airport at Port Moresby, the capital, looks ultra-remote. This is a different place than anything I have ever experienced. It feels like we have landed on another planet, beyond our known world.

They herded us into the first waiting area to be processed, or vetted. When we stepped through the door, we saw up on the wall a large sign MALARIA ENDEMIC.

Oh great! Being a missionary is a little like marriage when you say, "I do," it is like a blank check with a signed signature…for richer or poorer, in sickness or in health. In reality, isn't that what God requires of discipleship? He signed His signature with His blood as Jehovah Jireh…He who provides rams (needs) in the thickets, if and when we need them.

Larry finished filling out all the registration forms, and when they learned we were going to Pabarabuk, they didn't even check through our luggage at customs. The Bible School at Pabarabuk, which is our destination, has a good reputation and is well known over the island.

Larry finished the paperwork, and then the man behind the counter said to my husband, "She (pointing at me) is going to have to be quarantined."

"What? Why? What have I done?"

"That orchid in your hair," the man told me.

"Oh, that. Here, take it. It's only something I picked up in the lobby of the Hong Kong airport."

With that, he was okay, and then he took us down through long hallways and corridors around to the checkout desk for Air Niugini. This was to be our last plane to whisk us up and over the mountains to our new tropical home in the jungles.

Here we are, waiting in the lobby for our "flight final" to Mount Hagen. *I feel like I could blow dust; I'm so thirsty.*

We have been warned at different times to NOT drink the water. I can certainly identify with the elderly fellow on the plane except all I wanted was water – WATER! I have to have something wet for my mouth.

We looked around and all we could find was sweet orange Fanta. "But I don't want that sweet stuff. Okay, I surrender, whatever, it is moist and wet." I'd like a little water too—to wash my hands.

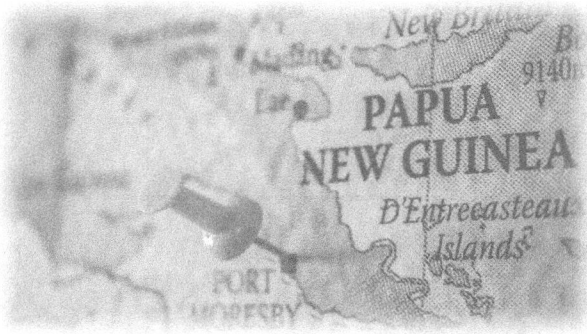

5: Our First Encounters

This is our first real encounter with the extremely friendly yet unkempt natives. A smiling little man volunteered to carry our luggage for us. He is looking out for our welfare. *He is so glad to see us here. That is why he is so willing to help us.*

Naïve we were…naive. Eight years later and more informed, that interpretation is different. We didn't know then the cultural thinking, or the art of paying for every kind of deed.

The Air Niugini plane waiting to fly us up over the mountains is much smaller than the one that brought us across the expanse of the ocean. The plane is filled with mostly nationals, and why not, it is their place.

It is 2:00 p.m. PNG time, which is really in conflict with our body's time.

The two female national flight attendants are dressed in Papua New Guinea's colors; black and red dresses decorated with the beautiful plumage of PNG's Bird of Paradise.

I'll have to say, that pilot is taking us for "a ride on the clouds."

All of a sudden, we felt the plane whirling down like a plane out of control. The pilot had found a hole and went for it. We all went spiraling around and down as if riding an amusement park ride, except we kept going. Thank God for skilled pilots; we made it through. It was an exhilarating experience.

The seasoned pilot made a perfect landing. Jehovah Jireh! God provided again!

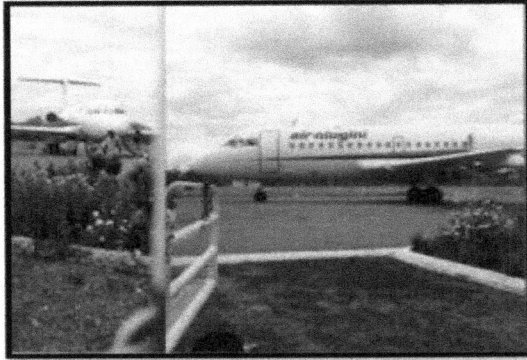

Air Niugini plane and airport

It is 4:00 p.m. just in time for this small, remote Mount Hagen airport to close, and we are three miles outside of town. No one is here to meet us, and we have no idea where to go. They are locking the doors behind us, and it's starting to rain.

Here we are standing outside of the closed terminal with all of our cargo, like four misplaced and unclaimed street urchins.

We watch the pilot put his gear into his chauffeured transport van. *He has been here before and knows his way around.*

The pilot is coming in our direction.

He asked my husband a few questions and then picked up our luggage and started loading it into his waiting van.

He said, "I bet no other pilot had loaded your baggage for you. Get in, we'll take you into town."

He is a kind man. This is where reality comes alive—how the Lord will take you up and give you beauty for ashes.

Jehovah Jireh equals *God looks after His own*. He put another ram in the bushes.

We snuggled inside the pilot's van. On our way into town we saw a woman sitting beside the road with a child bent over her parting the woman's black, curly hair. All of a sudden, the little girl pops her two thumbnails together. I assume she got it. One dead louse..."sure kill". This is becoming a common sight.

It didn't take us long to learn about lice—or other mites. How we process information is up to the cultural mindset. Robin, our teenage daughter said later, "If I get lice, I'll die. I'll just die." That is the American mindset. The battle of the mites in PNG is an established fact—without making one feel ostracized or rejected.

Here we are at our drop-off destination, Mapang Missionary Home, a place for missionaries to stay when they come into town. A Land Rover is parked in front of the Home. Two men, who resemble plain-clothed missionaries, are standing outside their vehicle. Could they be waiting for us?

They introduced themselves as Brother Daniel Glick, originally from Ohio, and Brother Glen Pelfrey, from Canada. Thank God! We have never met these missionaries before, but we feel a connection, like family that we didn't know we had.

We are going over dirt, gravel, and pothole roads toward Pabarabuk Station. We see near-naked, next-to-earth, underprivileged nationals walking out from the hills, down the road, and from seemingly everywhere waving and smiling showing their beautiful teeth. Nothing resembles the America we just left.

My first impression of this strange, never seen before culture, completely changed after we lived here a few days. I love them. Strange, but I felt a real love for the PNG people even before we came.

We are nearing the station on a challenging, narrow, red-clay road. The first house on the right is a black, two-story wooden structure that has been painted with black oil.

It is evening. The driver of the Land Rover pulled up in front of that black house, which was located at the front of the mission station, and the one man said, "This is your house."

I see and feel, yes, this is a mission field. They took us down a gully and back up onto the other side. There are beautiful flowers of different kinds growing all around, and the beautiful red Poinsettias stand tall as they crown the station. They are so beautiful!

Brother Glick said, "For now, you will stay at the Pelfrey's house, in the guest room. Brother Pelfrey is the station manager, and his wife Dorothy is the nurse supervisor at the clinic. They are conservative Canadians."

More than once we are reminded, "You are new (green) missionaries. New missionaries do not vote their first year on the field, they are to listen and learn."

Mostly native foods are available for us: pineapple, bananas, papayas, and *kaukau* sweet potatoes.

Being new, I don't think we appreciated these native foods like we would now.

For breakfast, we have sliced papayas, heavy bread, which occasionally is molded. The stove's open gas flame serves as our toaster. Butter, or rather a spread, comes from a can. It's tasteless, and it resembles yellow Crisco. It's supposed to take the place of good ole cow butter.

The smell of Dettol, the disinfectant that is used to wash the dishes, diffuses its pungent smell throughout the air with its own peculiar impression. Eating with these new smells is like...uh... new and different.

So this is what another country's culture is like? To me, it is like a whole different planet...beyond our previous world.

Jungle Beat

February 1977

It is the second month of the year and our second night in PNG. We are still trying to recover from jet lag.

Last night at bedtime we heard hollering, shouting, and what sounded like drums. In my tired mind, I envisioned a war dance, natives with bones in their noses, a large body-sized pot with boiling water ready for human soup. At least that is the way the movies were back in America.

Somewhere in time and our exhaustion, the jungle sounds drifted off into the distance. We slept soundly.

It's morning. What a peculiar feeling to wake up in a place we know little of, except what we have read about in books. Books did not let us smell PNG's own particular smell. It is not one I can honestly describe, but it feels good to be here, in the land of our calling. It reminds me of when God called Abraham to leave the land of his nativity to go out into an unknown country.

It feels mysteriously good to wake up as the sun is yawning its rays through the window of our room.

The discussion at the table this morning informed us that the sounds we heard last night were not drums or a dream; they came from discontented students rioting. They were saying that a select few students are unhappy because the Papua New Guinea Bible Institute (PNGBI) is unregistered with the government, even though they graduate students through grade 12, which is advanced for PNG where school is only offered until grade six.

The talk among the staff was that the PNGBI school has produced airline attendants, pilots, teachers, geologists, and government ministers, and one even became a PNG ambassador to the USA, living in a fancy house outside of Washington D.C. Still others have furthered their education in other countries. Employers say they are glad to have PNGBI graduates, especially the banks, because, "We can trust them."

A staff meeting continued till noon discussing the matter. The final conclusion is: the students knew about the registration when they came here to school.

- The school is here for those who cannot get into government schools.
- Many nationals are not privileged to attend public school after what they call, "grade six leavers." That is as far as the PNG government schools go, and school is not compulsory in PNG, at this time.
- They said the government developed a school for those who want to go on to grade ten; yet, the Pabarabuk Bible School graduates students all the way through grade twelve, if they want to go.

The climax was: the troublemakers were dismissed, disciplined, or they were disposed to settle in.

I am learning what the bare bones of medicine are. Larry went up to the "joinery and machine" shop to look around. He did more than look. He came back to the house bleeding. He showed me a "plumb-red," bleeding finger that he had ripped open on barbed wire.

Think…act…*there is no hospital to take him to for stitches. He had his tetanus shot before we came*, of course, that doesn't suffice in the case of infection or blood poisoning.

He came into the Pelfrey's washroom where I washed off the blood to assess the situation. It looked savable. I applied Sister Pelfrey's antibiotic powder, which is used generously in PNG, and Bacitracin salve, which I had brought with me. I cut regular Band-Aids in the form of butterfly Band-Aids and pulled the skin snuggly together. Then I wrapped it with torn strips of old sheets, and off he went to heal, which he did, beautifully.

Several years later the Pelfreys left PNG and went to Russia, where Sister Pelfrey died. Brother Pelfrey then went to Belize as a missionary, where he later died.

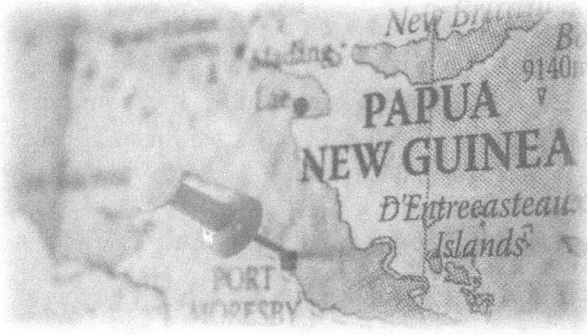

6: Foreign Physicals

March 1, 1977

Dear Diary: This is the first day that I am to give physicals and teach health…that foreign language. Our checklist for physicals is lice, leprosy, tinea (ringworm), scabies, dermatitis, dental caries, or whatever else needs attention for better health.

I am learning the word "only." Milk is "only" for babies, and it makes big folks sick. Shoes are "only" for Westerners and Europeans.

We have been here a couple of weeks and we need food. We also need something to stave off those pesky malaria mosquitoes.

Pulled Over

March 5, 1977

Larry, Robin, Mendy, and I got a ride on our mission bus to go into town for supplies and mosquito nets. On our way in, about one mile out of town, the police pulled the mission bus over for a road check. We learned at that time our bus lacked sufficient papers, because the police had not provided sufficient papers previously. All of us on the bus had to walk the rest of the way into town. All that is, except the driver who stayed with the bus, and the two young men who trekked miles back to the mission to get other transportation.

Among my first purchases were Camoquin, an antimalarial for Melinda, our youngest daughter, and mosquito nets. It is common for Europeans (that is what they call white people) to take malarial prophylactics from the Chemist, which we call pharmacists.

Whooping Cough, Horse Milk and Scabies

March 18, 1977

> We use whatever medication we have on hand that may help with the symptoms.

We have six in-patients in the clinic today. Three infants have the symptoms of whooping cough; spastic dry coughs in continuous succession, lasting for short periods of time. We use whatever medication we have on hand that may help with the symptoms. Mothers in the Highlands have little information on prevention and health care. It is a daunting task to educate those who know little about germs.

My mother told me I had whooping cough when I was a child. I don't remember it, but she said she gave me horse milk as treatment. We have no horse milk here, besides, I don't think that would go over very well, so we treat with whatever we have, be it outdated or not. It is common to have only outdated medication on hand, and yes, PNG has socialized medicine.

Penicillin and sulfa drugs are the government's medicines of choice. The idea here in the highlands is that Penicillin is a cure-all. They even give "shuts" shots to their ailing pigs, if they can get hold of the Penicillin and syringe.

People come to us for a "shut" for scabies. Of course, when they scratch, especially with hands that are soiled, that leaves the skin open to infection and the need for antibiotics. Some children are covered with sores from scratching their scabies.

We have a regular scale clinic where Mums bring their little ones to get weighed and get their immunizations. It also gives the younger ones a record of their birth so they know their age and have a record of their immunizations. That's progress.

Many of the older folks do not know when they were born or their age. They pick a date and claim that for their birthdate. Miss Lenita, the missionary at Kaupena, has a record of the ones that are born, at least the ones she knows of.

In our early preparation days for Papua New Guinea, I was told mothers in Papua New Guinea did not care for their babies, but this momma proved that a misstatement. Momma appeared to be in agony with tears streaming down her dark, red cheeks. I knew this momma carried a mother's love like any other mother in our world.

Prenatal, Hepatitis, and Scorpions

Today, a new mother-to-be had her first prenatal exam. This is a common procedure in America, but to these ladies, it is a foreign intrusion; therefore, it did not continue as a regular procedure here in PNG. Thank the Lord for my much-needed experience at Cabell Huntington Hospital in Huntington, West Virginia in obstetrics of labor, delivery, and post-partum.

Another woman came in from the bush coughing with blood in her sputum and high temperatures. From the description of her complaints, we suspected tuberculosis. She got a written pass to go on to Mt. Hagen Hospital for tests.

When sick cases are beyond our capabilities, we send them on to Mt. Hagen Hospital, whose main doctor is Doctor Bevis from Australia.

The generator just went off, which means it's 9:00 p.m., and I am now writing this under the mosquito net using a *torch* flashlight.

Hepatitis has been showing up in the area. We mainly treat the symptoms: fever, pain, lack of appetite, nausea, vomiting, and jaundice and try to teach prevention.

Robin and her three missionary friends were playing Monopoly at our house when the boy of Canadian missionaries made this announcement, "They think I might have hepatitis."

What else can we do? He is here. So they went on with the game and refreshments. Here in the wilderness, travesties are met if and when they come. We are learning to worry less about them, and just work through them, when, and if they do come. As the song goes, "We Just Keep Trusting the Lord."

A few days later, we learned that the Canadian boy does have hepatitis. He is an active teenager who refuses to let hepatitis slow him down, or to be quarantined. Thank the Lord, we never heard of anyone else from that social time that contracted the febrile disease from the teenager.

Oh yes, today we killed a scorpion running across the kitchen sink cabinet with his tail up in a curl. At the end of its tail or telson is where its venom is produced. Its tail continues in five separate divisions out from its abdomen. Toward the tip of its tail is a sharp needle-like projection called aculeus. We have found them climbing our bedroom wall and one coming out from under the chair where someone was sitting.

People tell us they come from the pineapple garden behind our house. They can show up most anywhere at any time, like unexpected guests. That scorpion was not the only thing that came to visit.

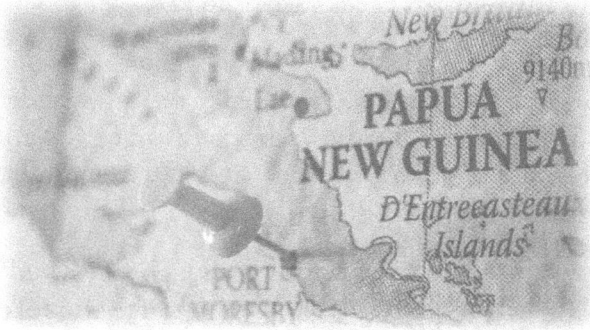

7: No, Not My Camera

March 30, 1977

Several medical missionaries from other stations and I are attending a Maternal and Child Health national workshop at Mt. Hagen Hospital. I am staying in Mapang. It feels so good to sit down to a fine meal prepared by someone else and to have a nice warm shower. Mapang is across the street from where the workshop is in session.

The class on Food Preparation is in the Nutrition Ward, which is an old 14' X 12' bush house made of pit-pit. Mums and babies sit around on the dirt floor while teachers show them how to put peanuts, *kaukau* sweet potatoes, *kumus* greens, and other tropical foods inside of a two-foot hollow bamboo rod to cook. After it is cooked, they pour it out onto a wide, green banana leaf, which they use like we use disposable plates in America.

I took a picture of a mother sitting on the ground in the cool of the morning, washing her baby. The naked baby shivered as the cool water ran down over her back into the wash pan. As the song goes, "This is the way we wash our babies."

Another stop was the national hospital ward where around ten wooden beds lined the walls accommodating sick patients, who were required to furnish their own food and bedding. Usually, a relative stays near to help with the patient's personal needs such as food.

One man was put outside in his hospital bed, out in the open air, in traction. I supposed it was traction. I stopped to see this wonder. I walked up to see what they had in the beat-up bucket hanging over the top of the foot of his bed. The bucket contained simple rocks inside that served as weights—so simple yet it works.

> I may not have known what he was talking about, but I knew...he was an angry man.

I thought this would make a nice picture for the folks back home in the USA to see, so I got out my camera and took his picture. When I started to leave, the patient's friend, standing beside the patient, talked to me in a language unknown to me. I may not have known what he was talking about, but I knew by his gruff reactions, body language, and facial expressions that he was an angry man. At least that is what he wanted me to believe.

I didn't know what to do or where this would lead. I got my picture and now it was time to get out of there. But the talker-stalker jabbered on acting like he could take my camera from me. I figured out the talker/stalker wanted money, or my camera. My camera wasn't an expensive one, but he sure wasn't going to get it from this American creature, just because I took a man's picture. And it was beyond my American intellect to pay for taking a public picture.

I see things differently now. I could have given the man a few Kenas PNG dollars. What would it have hurt?

The other pictures I had on the camera were unusual and one of a kind, but I didn't fuss with him. I just started walking toward where the rest of the health group was assembled. I walked. He walked. When I got close to the group, one of the national fellows of the health group walked over to the stalker and said something to him, indistinguishable to me. The stalker turned around and left. I really do thank God again for the protection of His guardian angel…Jehovah Jireh.

A Vine Wrapped Stretcher

April 17

We were ready for Sunday school at 9:00 a.m. when four village men came carrying their sister onto the station on a makeshift stretcher made by wrapping vines around and around 2 poles. They wanted me to go to the clinic. They said, their sister had no *pispis* urine or *pekpek* bowel movement for twelve weeks. That sounded like miscommunication somewhere along the line, but she needed more than our little clinic was prepared for, so they hired a truck, which took them with their sister to Mount Hagen Hospital.

April 18

Larry went to Christian Leadership Training College (CLTC), a farm beyond Mount Hagen to purchase baby chicks. This was his first time driving from the right side of the van to the left side of the road.

Our two girls did their school. Mendy's little black kitten is missing. We were told people here like to eat cats. She is feeling despondent.

A village man came to my door about 3:00 p.m. with a note from Sister Pelfrey, which said, "This man's wife is in hard labor. Can you come over to the clinic?"

The woman did have hard labor, and finally, the precious little dark-skinned bundle was born at 5:00 p.m. Sister Pelfrey sutured the new mother's perineal tear, while I attended to the baby with a low Apgar rating. I used a bulb syringe to clear the airway, and then I rubbed the baby all over to improve its circulation. Then I wrapped the baby in a blanket and laid her on her mother's belly to nurse, which helps the mother's fundus to contract by expressing the unneeded blood of the uterus, which in turn promotes a firmer fundus and speedier healing.

Larry finally got home from CLTC after dark. He walked over to the mechanic shop, looked down, and there was Mendy's little black kitten. Needless to say, she was happy. The lost is found, and the baby chicks are doing fine. Our happiness continues…

Robin had been praying for $10.00. When Larry brought the mail in from Mount Hagen, there was a letter from Mrs. Doubledee in the states, a returned missionary after being in Africa for twenty years. In the letter was $10.00. It has been a happy day. *Jehovah Jireh* equals *God provides* again.

April 19

When I woke up this morning, I couldn't talk—laryngitis?

We came by another cooking stove, so I made biscuits and gravy. After our family finished eating, I went to class. I could barely talk; strange how I made progress with the students today.

Mendy woke up this morning with severe stomach pains. There are so many respiratory and intestinal problems in PNG. Our water comes from rain that drains off the metal roof of our house, down into a galvanized tank, and then into the house through pipes.

Clean water is always questionable. When we first came to PNG we were warned to always boil our water. That soon got old, so we stopped.

We have rainy seasons that help to keep water fresher, and then we have dry seasons. Without fresh water, there is always a threat to health. It is no wonder sickness uses the island as a resort.

Respiratory infections are frequent. The younger generations are not used to cleaning the nasal passages in a sanitary way. It is common to see green, nasal mucus curds hang where a mustache rests. Then there are those who wipe their nose and rub it into their skin. This is contrary to our American way of wiping the nose on a handkerchief and sticking it in our pockets. The nationals ask, "Why do you keep it in your pocket?" That was a question I hadn't thought of before; because that is the way we Americans have always done it, at least where I was raised in Ohio.

Larry went to Mt. Hagen town today for supplies. He called his mother all the way over to America, to Wild and Wonderful West Virginia. Bless her heart, she kept saying, "I'm so nervous I don't know what to say." She is a great supporter of her prayers.

At noon I went home, got dinner, taught Mendy, and made a cake. By 3:00 p.m. I was in class at the clinic and checked on the new baby that was born yesterday. Someone had removed the umbilical clamp and put a dirty string in the place of it. I suppose they preferred the string to that yellow, weird-looking hard plastic that didn't fit with their inherited way of thinking. Isn't that the way we are too? We stay pretty much with what we have been taught.

Midnight Delivery

April 24

This Sunday has been a full day. We went to an outstation for church services and returned extremely tired. Before I got home, a woman came and wanted me to look at her baby. Babies can come in all colors, but they all come with little gas bubbles in their tummies.

Today in the clinic, I removed a new mama's stitches so she could be discharged. Her granddad had died. She was weeping and wanted to go home.

We use whatever kind of sutures we can get, and they may not all be absorbable.

On our way home from church, Wai, our mission national truck driver, came telling me something, which I had difficulty understanding. I finally figured out he was saying his wife was ready to *karim pikinini* have her baby. Larry took Mendy on over to church with him, while Robin and I went off to the clinic, in the dark.

In America, it is common practice that when a woman is ready for delivery, she goes to the hospital. In PNG this is a new concept; therefore, many still choose to deliver down at the river. Wai's wife, being associated with the mission, was more open to coming to the clinic to have her baby, plus it was night.

Sister Pelfrey came over to the clinic, and we transferred a new mother out of the labor and delivery room into another room. We put Wai's wife in the examining/labor room. Sure enough, she was in labor.

Our labor room has plywood floor and walls, and a simple wood-slat cot. Our delivery supplies are nature's best…like in the old days of America; only we didn't boil the water.

Later someone asked, "Why didn't you boil the water?" Answers to that question vary with individuals.

1. One reason for boiling water is to give the dad something to do to keep him occupied.

2. Mothers like to put a warm soak on their perineal area.

3. Warm water works better to clean the birthing equipment and for bathing the mother and baby.

There are other reasons for or against boiling water for a delivery by different individuals, but boiling water for a delivery is not a dictate. You cannot put your hands or the baby into boiling water.

I admit, warm water would be helpful, but we had no way of getting either in this bush clinic at night.

The Papua New Guinea Highland woman's custom, in advanced labor, is to get down on her hands and knees on the floor in knee-chest position. When her contractions increase with pain, she rocks back and forth. Gravity is not their friend in this position. We strongly encouraged them to get up onto the wooden cot and off the floor…the American way, at least right before delivery.

It is not the easiest thing for the nurse to get down on the floor trying to assist the mother in an awkward position as she is in labor and ready for delivery. I was able to convince some to try it our way for a smoother delivery—at least from our point of view.

It soon was time for the men to shut down the generator. It shuts off for the whole mission station at 9:30 every night. Then all we have is our candlelight, kerosene lamp, and our hand held, 6-volt sealed beam. They are nothing to compare with the big beams that shine down from the ceiling of operating theaters in America, but that is not our luxury.

After a time, we were able to coax Wai's wife to get onto the wooden cot, while Robin, tired as she was, stood like the "lady of liberty" holding the 6-volt battery light over us. We worked with the miracle in the process.

The new mamma delivered an eight-pound boy at 11:30 p.m. after a hard labor. Isn't that what most labors are? I've heard of easy labor, but I have not seen one. We stayed until Mamma and baby were doing fine and appeared comfortable.

We returned back to our houses at 1:00 a.m.

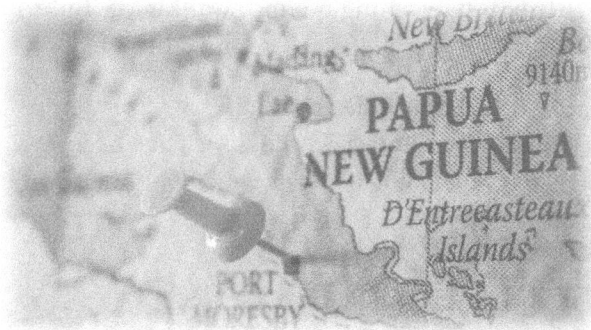

8: Earth is Finished

April 24

It was off to teach school as usual until noon. After lunch, I worked with Mendy at her school in our house. While she was doing her lessons, the earth began to tremble and then it shook. It was a strong earthquake! Things began to move around in the schoolroom. When I looked over at Mendy, she was pale. The pink color had drained from her face.

In her six-year-old mind, she remembered the accounts in the Bible that tell about the end of the earth, and she thought this was it. When the "quaking" began to subside, I tried to encourage her by saying, "It's over."

Mendy looked even more frightened. White veiled her face. She said softly, "It is?" She thought I meant the earth was finished. That was a true emotional "earthshaking" moment for her until I explained what I meant.

Later in the day, I was getting ready to go back to the clinic to teach, when I heard a woman wailing. It was coming from the clinic. When I got there, I saw a mother holding a very sick two-year-old child in her arms. The child was still breathing. I motioned for the mama to bring the child to the room where we kept the oxygen tank, like the ones used in the joinery shop. She came up to the door, but she wouldn't bring the child in.

The papa came over, took the sick child, and carried it back toward the village with the mamma trailing behind, wailing pitifully. I was told they wanted to get back to the village before the child died.

This evening I worked on grades, while Larry wrote letters to family and friends back home. The knocks on the door have been many. The generator went off, lights out, and I'm still working on grades, but I must go to bed. I am so sleepy.

Up the Chimney We Went

May 1

Today is school break. We borrowed our Pabarabuk Station's truck and rode for two and a half hours over rough mountain terrain to take students from their Pabarabuk dorms to each of their villages. We let each of them off at the road, or path, which took them back to their village.

Larry drove on to the Tambul Mission Station, which has a Tok Pisin Bible school. We stayed with missionary friends who wanted to take us deeper into the bush to one of the mission's outstations.

Nolene Haynes and me in pig mire.

Morning came. We trekked (that's an understatement) to an outstation. It was a good thing I wore my knee socks and heavy shoes with thick soles. We climbed over fences and waded through a valley swamp of pig mire, which went up almost to our knees. Nolene Haynes, a missionary friend, took her shoes and socks off to wade through the mire.

I said, "No way am I taking mine off. Only the good Lord knows what is beneath all of this muck…broken glass, sharp rocks, or there could be anything." I could see with my mind's eye all the bacteria that lay-in-

waiting beneath to introduce disaster—more than we already had.

Larry coming up through the chimney

We slid, waded, and stumbled up the mountain and then squeezed up through a small narrow passage through a rock known as "the chimney." I will have to admit that I was somewhat claustrophobic. After we shimmied up through the narrow hole of the rock, we climbed up the rest of the mountain until we arrived at a remote village where one of our school students stood waiting for us in front of the church.

The small church had only one opening, a door where you had to bend over and step over boards to go inside where the only light was what crept through the pitpit and small door. People gathered to worship, not in a glass cathedral, but in a humble sanctuary, compliments of Mother Nature. However, the darkness, after a long hard trek, and not understanding the language did nothing to help us stay awake.

When Church was over, we shook hands, took pictures, and said our goodbyes. It was time for the downward descent – without a guide. This time we went in another direction to get back to the Tambul Mission Station. The Haynes and Gray families climbed, stumbled, fell, waded, slid, and puffed their way back.

This is the way we go to church: Larry, Mendy, myself and Robin. The church with the grass roof is behind us.

We came to a stream of water. Everyone except me had crossed over. After Larry jumped over, he reached out his hand to help me with my jump. Holding my hand tight, he gave a jerk when I was not ready, and I ended up right in the water. Of course, I accused him of pulling me in, and the other couple continues to laugh about it, to this day. *I still don't think it was funny.*

Back at the station, we washed the best we could, disinfected ourselves, and washed our shoes. I attended to my skinned legs and then it was time to get something to eat.

Later, we heard a ruckus brewing outside on the Tambul station. The national male students were refusing to eat the food the national women had fixed. On further investigation, we learned when a female has her *mun sik* menstrual period, men will not eat the food she has prepared. (I am still trying to figure out how the men know when a girl has a period.) Men believe they will shrink like a prune, to a weak diddlysquat of a man.

That belief, the station manager will have to work out with the male students. When I was a girl, my dad would say, 'A person convinced against their will is of the same opinion still.'

Tonight, Larry preached at the Tambul Pidgin Bible School Church on how Jesus suffered for each of us, to forgive our sins and free us from a guilty conscience, and how He salvages us from the devil and his fiery place called hell. After the service, a man came to Larry with tears of joy. He said, "I liked your message, now I feel real joy in my heart.

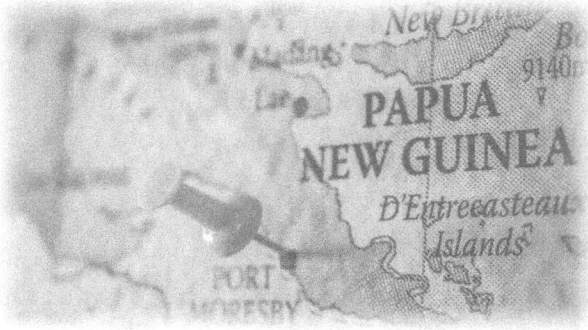

9: Leprosy and Chicken Pox

May 6

Back to Pabarabuk: Today looks like it is going to be a big day. I went to the clinic early this morning, and Daniel, our trained national "doctor boy," is away for three days. I organized and updated medical records when I wasn't tending to the sick.

There are many people sick with unusual and interesting cases such as leprosy. We check to see they are taking their medication, and we observe their skin. We had patients with pneumonia, chicken pox, skin infections, boils, high temperatures, and more.

I managed to get home in time to put together a double batch of rolls for supper and then back to the clinic.

It is so important to have a good *tainim tok* interpreter to talk for us in the people's own language. That is an integral part of helping people.

I marvel at how God helps a common nurse like me work with challenging illnesses. Now, I realize that nurses in America are capable of performing more duties than they are allowed to do by law, especially when God is there guiding them.

The Bible says the Holy Spirit will teach you all things. That means you can't go wrong with supernatural teaching.

I managed to get home about 5:00 p.m. in time to help Dorcas, a student who works for us as part of her schooling, since Robin is not feeling well.

This is fortnight, when Larry, the newly appointed station manager, pays the workers for working in the mission's coffee gardens. Coffee is what helps to finance the school, and it teaches students a vocation.

It seems Larry will never get home for supper.

Afterward, it was bathe Mendy, make a one-hour tape to send back home, take a shower, and get enough water for Larry to bathe. Once again, the day ended with me writing in my diary by candlelight. I can hardly see. Larry is in the office counting out the school's money to deposit in the bank in the morning.

This is the way we wash our clothes

Robin is a big help in the clinic, with the national children, and at home. She takes our dirty laundry outside with a big, red, plastic type of dish-pan and uses a little washboard we brought from the states, on which to scrub our clothes. That washboard is a luxury. Before that, I scrubbed our clothes in the kitchen sink using the deep treads on the sole of my rubber boot. Both methods are hard on the knuckles, but it works when it is all you have.

Robin washing our clothes on a scrub board.

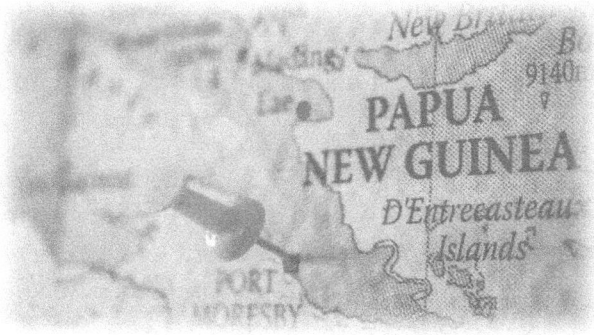

10: Rolling in the Dough

March 7

Eating hot, buttery, homemade bread is an experience, and making it can be another.

Today, I made bread using Grandma Giltner's recipe. She's an elderly lady we met at the mission's headquarters in Summerfield, Florida before we left the states.

In the making, I had dough everywhere: two large loaves, four small loaves, half pan of rolls, a half pan of cinnamon rolls, and a dish of yummy cheese rolls.

They were all spread out like a small yeast army with their aroma circling up into the air as if ready for battle. I could hardly wait for them to stand up tall enough to go into the oven.

Our apartment size stove that was left in the house by another missionary is a gas stove and different from the stoves I have been used to. The oven's flame blazes up in the back of the inside of the oven, and the oven has no temperature control.

The dough finally looked ready. I put two loaves into the oven and set the faulty control dial.

Later, it was not a dial that alerted me, but it was my nose indicating that I better look inside the oven. Oh no! There were two dark, chocolate brown loaves of bread, instead of the golden brown I was looking for; neither were they chocolate. I had all of this dough and no good oven to bake it in.

> Commodities here are not plentiful. We only go to get supplies when someone else happens to be going into town...

Commodities here are not plentiful. We only go to get supplies when someone else happens to be going into town, which is not often.

Life is still new for us. We are trying to adjust to yellow butter in a can, which looks and tastes like yellow Crisco, it could be. Our milk is a dry powder that comes in a twenty-five-pound bag. It is not instant, and extremely difficult to mix if it mixes at all, but we are blessed to even have lumpy powdered milk to drink or use.

"What do I do now?" I took the challenge and went to Esther Hershey, our missionary neighbor's house, to see if I could perchance use her oven if she wasn't using it.

She said, "There it is."

The rest of the bread dough baked just perfectly. That hot buttery goodness was a delight.

From my diary: *"Had a hard day; felt like I'd rolled in the dough all day."*

When It Rains, It Pours

May 13

Missionaries came into Pabarabuk from all our surrounding mission stations for the yearly missionary conference. People are accommodated in the seven houses of Pabarabuk missionaries' homes. The wives are doing the cooking, and the men eat hearty with no complaints. The conference has been in session for several days.

Today, the Lord's presence was so real. This afternoon, however, Brother Antrim read the scriptures; Brother Pelton began to cough. He began having symptoms of a heart attack. Nolene, from the Tambul Mission, and I laid him down on the floor and began working with him. We have no heart monitors, and no modern equipment to work with, so we monitored his vitals, loosened his constricting buttons, and tried to provide as much oxygen as possible. After a time, he began to recover, and then the men moved him over to the Taylor's missionary house.

While we were at the Taylor's with Brother Pelton, a missionary boy came running and said, "Brother Gray fell and hurt his head; he wants you to come home."

I went up and across the valley to our house to investigate. Larry had climbed to the top of the walled bookcase and fell, bruising his side, and putting a big "bump knot" on his face.

Later, Beverly, Kaupena's mission nurse, and I went to the clinic to try to locate more medicine for Brother Pelton.

I suppose the devil sensed God was in this place, and he couldn't stand it. Tonight, the Lord's Spirit came into our presence in a mighty way. His presence was really manifested, like outstanding! People laughed, cried, and testified. Some of the missionary children and teenagers committed their lives to Jesus to live for Him. We didn't get home until 11:00 p.m.

"Praise God from whom all blessings flow. Praise Him all creatures here below." The Lord is my song, and He furnishes refreshing living water to the thirsty spirit of mankind.

Both Brother Pelton and Larry recovered. God, Jehovah Jireh, provided more rams in the thicket.

May 17

Missionary folk left yesterday to go home from the mission conference.

It's back to school again. Before the second-period class, Donald and Peggy Broniman from the Pulapatu mission station brought their mother to my house and wanted me to look her over. They were on their way back from the conference to Pulapatu when she began feeling sick.

The final decision was made to take her to a Nazarene Hospital at Kujup, which was about a two and a half hour drive on the other side of Mount Hagen. Since transportation is hard to come by, and I had been having pain in my right side, it worked out for me to go with Sister Broniman. The doctor referred us both to Goroka Hospital, about one hundred and thirty miles from home over high mountains and treacherous dirt roads.

Doctor Teague, at Goroka, admitted Sister Broniman to the hospital for observation and diagnostic testing. I sat beside her bed in the outmoded ward and watched as the cleaning lady mopped the cement floors. She took a bucket of water and scattered it on the floor, and then she took a mop and mopped up the water. I learned there is more than one way to mop a floor.

That got me thinking. I now have a squirt bottle of water, and I spray my wood and vinyl floors and then mop and clean it up. It works great for me.

Thanks to the cleaning lady in the out-of-times hospital. I learned a lot from the nationals I went to teach.

At night, I stayed at the Swiss Mission close to the hospital.

Sister Broniman had a series of X-rays, but nothing serious or worthy of surgery was detected.

Before we left, the doctor who examined me said my problems were:

1. I could have the beginning of an ulcer in the duodenal area, or
2. My pain could be from spasms of the intestines.

He prescribed antacid tablets and antispasmodic medication. It helps when I take them. I am not much for taking medicine, but neither am I much for pain.

Sister Broniman was released and we headed back toward our Pabarabuk Station.

On our way toward home, Sister Broniman lay in the back seat of the van while we pushed on through steep mountains with tropical rains.

A big ATA shipping truck was stuck in the mud on the side of a mountain. We gave one of the drivers a ride up the road to where he could get help. Farther up the road was an earth-moving caterpillar on its side, suspended onto the side of the mountain. If the dirt beneath it would move a little, that mammoth would come tumbling down onto the road below, and maybe on down.

These mountains are so steep that brakes burn out easily from overuse. It is not uncommon to pass stalled trucks where men had burned their brakes out while braking down the mountain.

We got back to the station around 9:00 p.m., just before the generator shut down and the lights went out. I'm so glad to be back home on the station.

May 22

This morning, Mendy woke up again with severe pains in her stomach. She asked us to pray for her. We did. Her pain continued. She asked, "Will you pray for me again?" We prayed the second time. She had one more spastic stomach pain. Now she's up and acts like nothing was ever wrong with her. Actually, she seems to have more energy than usual.

This morning, Mendy woke up again with severe pains in her stomach.

Praise the Lord for answered prayer. He is our emergency room physician. He is The Physician who heals completely and does not only treat symptoms.

Bike Calamity

May 27

"This is a beautiful day, and there is no clinic class today with students. It seems like my day off."

Since it is such a nice day, I went over to missionaries Esther Hershey and Marie Trapani's house across the road from us. There in their front yard was a small motorbike. *That looks like fun. The day is so lovely. I think I will take a ride.* Never mind that I had never ridden a motorbike before, but no problem. *It is such a nice day for a ride.*

I straddled the motored apparatus and found the on switch. *Now what do I do? Take off, that is all you have to do.* I accelerated the gas, and it took off. It was my first participation in a bike rodeo.

I tried going between Esther's steps and flowers, but instead, I ran into the steps. That means I was half on and halfway off the bike with the motorbike still running. I couldn't get it shut off. I did so hope no one was watching. I looked like Mary Poppins in a dilemma.

I survived with just a bruise on my leg and an extra supply of adrenalin. I left the bike in its rightful yard and back to our house I went. I figured I needed a little more practice.

May 30

It is Memorial Day in the USA, but here, it is school as usual. Today is unusually cool for the tropics.

A clinic student came to me and said a baby was crying severely. I went to the clinic to check on it. I noticed it was passing flatus, which is a gas that is passed from the intestines. Belly pain can be caused by swallowing air, or from something ingested, or by bacterial fermentation in the digestive system.

I gave the baby Chloral Hydrate, which is according to medical protocol here in PNG. I laid the baby across my lap on its stomach, like I had done for my three babies, and it stopped crying almost immediately. The nationals stood in amazement. I prayed and then thanked God for the confidence in prayer that He may have received from this.

Excitement Charged the Air

June 1

While waiting for the family to come home to eat, I looked out the window and saw something rather unusual. A crowd of people gathered out in front of our house on the road. I went to see what was stirring them. Robin met me and told me what happened,

"This morning a pig got into the school garden (which is the source of food for the school), and Brother Glick and a few nationals caught the pig and put it in *kalabus* jail. Late this evening, the papa of the pig broke the lock to get into the building to retrieve his pig. Brother Glick saw the man and went to get the pig back from him since the man was responsible for the damage his pig had caused. That is the 'law of the pig' in PNG. The man pulled at the rope, while Brother Glick held onto the man. The man got away, ran up the road, and found a good place to fall over—right in front of our house."

The atmosphere is electrically charged with excitement and high emotions. Nationals are singing out across the valley, *"Glick em kilim wanpela man, Glick em kilim wanpela man."* Glick killed a man. Glick killed a man. This could mean death for Brother Glick and maybe for the rest of us…an eye for an eye law.

The atmosphere is electrically charged with excitement and high emotions.

The darkness of night settled in. Robin went into the house to get a *torch* flashlight. I went out and bent over the immobilized man to assess the situation.

Robin handed me the light and I shined it on him. His eyes were shut. I noticed that when the light beamed in on his eyelids he squinted. Then I noticed he moved his muscles. He could not hold completely still. All the while, he was trying to make the people think he was dead. I leaned over him and tried to raise his eyelids, but he squeezed his eyes together. Aw-ha! He then rolled his eyes up and back into his head. The people standing around saw that he was not dead.

A few of the fellows then picked him up and carried him over to the clinic to Daniel, our national doctor boy.

It was told later that after all his spectators left the clinic, he got up and was laughing about what he had done. That made his tribesmen angry, because they were almost ready to kill missionary Glick. Had the killing frenzy started only the Lord knows where it would have stopped. Yes, only the Lord knows.

Recently, back in America, recently we were told the nationals still talk about how they thought Brother Glick really had killed the national.

June 14

Larry has a cold, but he drove to Mt. Hagen in the 3-ton Fuso truck known as the "6000" for its weight. He took coffee in to sell, but he got only 1 Kena and 13 toea per pound, which would be about 79 cents in American money, at this time. The price of coffee is down.

He went to get supplies for us and found sausages for the first time in Mt. Hagen. He also got mince ground beef, gravy beef, flour, bread, and baking powder. Brother Glick and Sister Pelfrey also went with him for supplies.

Later, Sister Pelfrey lost her liver she bought. She said, "Larry put it in the truck while I was standing there. When I got home I couldn't find it." I feel sorry for them. It is no easy task to get to town, and it is certainly no easy task to buy supplies and to get them home.

You don't dare leave your vehicle unattended, especially in town.

It wouldn't surprise me if the devil got it to cause strife among the brethren. Anything to cause strife seems to be his business. The Apostle John wrote in the tenth chapter of his book, "The thief", meaning the devil "comes not, but for to steal, and to kill, and to destroy:" Jesus said, "I am come that they might have life and that they might have it more abundantly."

While Larry was in Mt. Hagen, I was in the classroom. Form 2 was so noisy and they disturbed the class so much that I dismissed them. They acted like they were whipped. My head was paining, and it was difficult for me to stand there and talk besides trying to talk over their noise. Some students came and apologized. Others came with sympathy and said those students bothered other classes too. I guess this is the time to take it to Brother Pelfrey, the principal.

I did manage to get through Form 1, and then I came home and went to bed. I didn't even go to the clinic class. Two missionary families came onto the station, but they by-passed our house.

Larry came in at about 5:15 p.m. He said, "I talked to one missionary family and they said they got no money again this month." This is an expensive place to live if you rely on buying supplies.

I also wrote to Sister Truman, a secretary at headquarters, back in Summerfield, Florida. On our monthly financial statements, the office has been paying bills that have already been paid, so I wrote to get that corrected.

One month we only got $30.00 in offerings. God bless the people who care and act on behalf of missionaries who are far away from home with no means of making money. The missionaries we know give their own sources to further the Kingdom of God.

Some nationals have commented how missionaries get a lot of money, but what many do not realize; the money that is sent to us goes back into Papua New Guinea. We do not make money here and then send it back home to the United States.

One national told me the people talk; they think missionaries come here with their suitcases full of money. She also told us there is an idea that all the money and goods really belonged to them at the beginning, and then the westerners came and took it from them. She told me they are called "the cargo cult." I read that there is also a group in Africa that thinks this way. In America, they call it entitlement.

I thank God for the Holy Spirit that can educate minds and teach them the truth…if people listen and heed it.

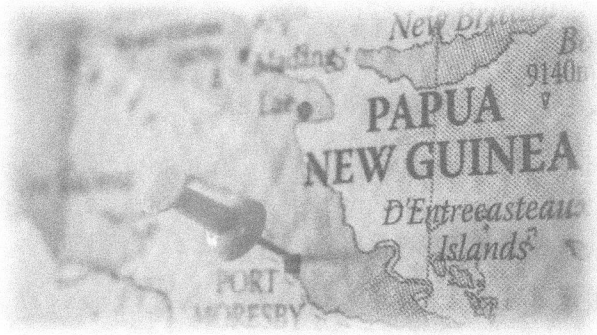

11: People Come and People Go

June 20

Pabarabuk is our mission's main station. We have a PNG school with about 400 students, and we can expect a flow of people coming and going almost anytime.

One missionary, from another station, came for advice about his wife who has excessive menstrual flow after having a dilatation and curettage (D & C) procedure.

Another family left.

Beverly, the single nurse from Kaupena Station, left this morning, after helping in our clinic till 10:00 a.m.

She came to our house depressed and crying saying she was the only missionary on her station and she needed help. She said she needed someone, a male—to man the Kaupena Station.

The Consecutive Executive Committee (CEC) scheduled a meeting to talk about moving us over to Kaupena to help her out.

Close to Now, Close to …

June 21

"Please, I don't want to see another mountain."

I had a restless night and today my throat is sore. I finished teaching at noon and went to our house to lie down on our wooden couch, which Brother Glick made from wood flooring.

It actually feels good to my aching bones. I feel so weak and tired.

I was there only a few minutes until I heard another knock on our door. It was a man from Kapaglami Village. He wanted help for his wife. A girl interpreted for me as he said in the Imbongu language that his wife had delivered yesterday, but she couldn't deliver the placenta.

I asked him if he would bring his wife to the clinic. He said, *mogul*—"No. The men are afraid of her.'"

The village men are afraid of a woman and her blood after she has delivered a baby or any woman's blood issues. They do not want to be emaciated, which they believed they would become after any kind of contact with a woman who has a blood flow.

I suggested that he get Bible School students to bring her to the clinic.

"She is ashamed and wouldn't come," he quietly said.

I got up from the couch and sent Mendy across the road to stay with Esther and Maria.

I sent for a few high school girls and a couple of high school boys to go with the village man, Robin, and me.

It was 1:30 p.m. when the six students, Robin, and I began our trek, which led us over a stream of water. Up—over—down and back up we went as we climbed our first mountain. I felt weak and sick and thought I could go no further.

The village man was supposed to be leading us, but he was used to the terrain and went on ahead, flitting over the mountains like a ghost.

Kepu, one of the schoolgirls, said she would "sing out" and ask the man to bring the woman to us, but for some undisclosed reason, that never happened. We climbed up and over, over and up, and used the roots of trees protruding out from the earth to get up parts of the side of the mountain.

Robin took one small bottle of water with her. Each time we stopped to rest, she wanted to take a drink. I encouraged her to save it as long as she could; we had much more terrain to cross. Down the path, I looked back and saw her sitting sipping water from the lid.

I asked the students, "How much farther?"

"Close to now, close to," they would say each of the several times I asked.

Over pig fences, around mountains, and finally, we were "close to." We had yet to go down and back up onto the next incline where the village man stood on the other side singing out for the students to take *ambo kandoli* the red/white woman back to the station…his wife is okay now.

You've got to be kidding me, just like that. I stood there in the foggy mist and asked my heavenly Father, "What do You want me to do? Did we come all of this way—through this toil for nothing?" After silent prayer, I felt the Lord would have me go onward.

> I stood there in the foggy mist and asked my heavenly Father, "What do You want me to do?"

Up the next incline, around the mountain, across several pig fences, onward through a muddy path, and stepping over brush covered with mud, we finally came to the little bush house on the side of what seemed like the tallest mountain around. We bent over to go through a four-foot door.

Three little naked children quietly ran around on the outside of what we would call a one-room home. Inside, overhead were herbs drying, or something dangling from the poles that were used for rafters. To my left and right were wall divides with boards over the dirt floor, which looked like where they possibly slept. Over against the right wall were stalls for seven pigs, however; only five portly-plump pigs occupied them. Two women sat around a fire that burned in the middle of the floor. One of the women sat with a newborn baby on her lap.

After a brief conversation, I examined the baby, cleaned the umbilicus with Zephiran, and sprinkled the umbilicus with antiseptic powder.

Before we left, and as we sat around the fire talking, the new mother confessed she didn't pray, meaning she wasn't a Christian. Before we left, we gave the mother a clean baby blanket, had prayer for her and the family, and then we left.

Also, before leaving, we took pictures of the children in front of the small door, and then we started that challenging trek home again, only this time, it was through the night, rain, and mud. We pulled and held on to each other to keep from sliding over the side of the mountain path.

Our path was narrow. Once, we looked up and saw a big razorback bush pig coming toward us. The PNG bush pigs can be ferocious. It is not uncommon for someone to come to the clinic to be sutured from a pig bite. The national students and Robin wasted no time getting out of its way. They jumped up on a steep bank beside us. That left the pig and me. As it got closer, I tried to jump on the bank too, but couldn't make it. One of the fellows put out his hand, gave me a big pull, and all of a sudden I was up on the embankment with the others—out of the pig's reach—"beautiful timing my guardian angel". *Jehovah Jireh* equals *the Lord provides.*

That I would say was another ram in the thickets!

On the way back to the station, we stopped to share a handful of cookies and crackers with eight people. My water didn't go far, to say the least, and I was so thirsty.

The night got darker and it started to rain again. The red PNG clay is as slippery as ice when it's wet. Robin's feet went out from beneath her several times and down she went—in the wet red clay. We returned back to the station on a lower trail; over the river and through the woods.

At last, off in the distance we saw the lights from the mission station. We headed in that direction—toward the lights of home.

We arrived back at our black oil-painted house at 7:30 p.m. We were worn out, tired, and thirsty. In PNG it is dusk at 6:30 p.m. and dawn at 6:30 a.m. year round. I plopped myself down on the couch. Later, I managed to get a shower to wash away the mud of forbearance. Afterward, we invited the students over for a hot cup of tea.

It's so good to be home. Please, I don't want to see another mountain for several days, or at all, the way I feel at this moment. I trust the Lord will use this trip somehow for His glory.

June 22

I had another restless night with chest pain. I greased my chest with Ben-Gay and got relief. I woke up so tired and sore I didn't feel like getting out of bed.

There was no school for Mendy today. I stayed in the house and didn't even go to clinic class. When I looked out the window at the beautiful mountains, I said, "I don't want to look at you today." I call this the "bare bones" of missionary nursing.

Voted Out to Another Station

Friday, June 24

The Church Executive Council (CEC) board voted for us to go to the Kaupena Station. Beverly Wickham is the only nurse at this time, and she says she needs help at the station. The clinic at Kaupena has been closed, the word is: because of a disagreement between two people in two countries; a leader in America and a leader in Papua New Guinea's Southern Highland's country. The board voted for Larry to be the station manager at Kaupena.

Hands off

There was a stir at the Pabarabuk School today. An older missionary who is used to discipline was teaching a class when one of the students started disturbing the class. The word came to us that she told him to leave the class and he wouldn't leave.

Troy and another person were sent to the police. The student resisted and fought the police. The missionary boy tried to help out the police by holding the student. I don't have to tell you that it went over like a lead balloon. The village people are really stirred. It's an unwritten "hands off" policy for Europeans or white people.

June 26

I have to share this with you. Sister Helen Glick, a missionary from Ohio, gave us a package of chocolate chips, and I made chocolate chip cookies. Treat! Treat! Treat! No, the chips were not a mirage. I made chocolate chip cookies for supper. They are real. They were tasty. They were a gift from heaven, a real treat.

Repercussions of the "Hands On"

June 30

Today, I felt the Lord's help as I had my last health class here at Pabara-buk.

This evening in a prayer meeting the discussion was on yesterday's incident of Pelfrey's son who held the disrupting student. A teacher from Kaga government school was there, and he said, "The Pelfreys might be in danger." He told us a group was coming down the road and he got in front of them and talked to them. There seems to be a big stir, certainly, this is not good, but God can undertake it for all concerned.

There are nationals who are prone to get stirred over the smallest matters. We just never know.

This third-world country is not unlike America where there is unrest, riots, and disorder.

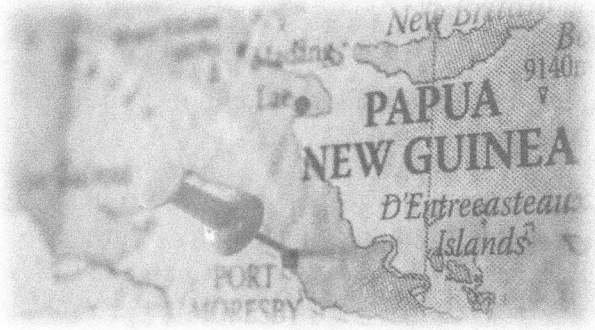

12: Not Yet

July 1

We are not going to Kaupena this weekend. We are waiting for Pilipo, a national who is returning from Bible College in America, to come and teach in Larry's place. Larry has been very busy with teaching and trying to take care of the farm while the usual national farmer men are gone. A pig somehow got her teats lacerated. One visiting pig is down in the back parts and one small pig died last night. The chickens have been dying, and there are pigs rooting in the coffee garden. Larry is a teacher, and even though he is a farmer at heart, he had to cancel his classes to take care of the farm until the regular farmers return.

July 2

We got word today that my paternal grandmother is dying of colon and liver cancer. It is hard to imagine her being so far away and I am not able to see her and hold her hand. When I was a girl, I watched Grandma Puckett as she combed her long gray hair, while sitting. It draped all the way to the floor. It was as long as a horse's tail. I asked her once, "Grandma, why is your hair so long?"

She said, "After Enos died, I didn't get it cut because of what people would say about me." Enos was my granddad that died in March 1918, two months before my dad was born. Grandma said, "In that day, for a woman to cut her hair, she was suspected to be a 'loose' woman." Grandma wore her hair long till her dying day.

I also remember staying with her, and for dinner, she fixed creamed corn. She knew I loved sweet creamed corn.

Then one time I stayed with her, I took a bath country style. Grandma had no running water, nor an inside bathroom, just a toilet way down over the hill where she kept old Sears or Montgomery Ward catalogs to clean off with. That was before the days of soft Charmin.

> One cold evening, she fixed a washtub of bath water and put it in the corner behind her wood/coal cook stove.

One cold evening, she fixed a washtub of bath water and put it in the corner behind her wood/coal cook stove. I climbed in and took a bath, there in the kitchen...sheltered by a hot stove.

She was a shouter too. I have seen my dear grandmother in the church so happy in the Lord that she would shout until her long, gray hair came down.

She was a good and gentle grandmother. Now she is dying; can I bring her back again? I shall go to her, but she will not return to me...on this earth.

We got more news today, from the other side of the world; my niece has a new baby.

One dies. One lives.

Moving Day

July 8

Well, this is the day. There seems to be no end to packing. We shipped only five barrels to PNG, but we have accumulated four truckloads of stuff to move. How can that be in a third world country? **Partly, because** my parents came through the great depression, so I learned to save "everything", and also because missionaries have been gracious to give. That's what missionaries do…give out that others may have.

Mendy and I went to the chapel to say, "so long." The students cried.

Dorcas, the girl who helped us in the house, and another student accompanied us over the river and through the woods to Kaupena. They will catch a public motor vehicle, a PMV bus, to return to Pabarabuk.

The children gathered around the goat we are keeping for another missionary. They really like it. It nibbled at one of the little boy's trousers—made of tanket leaves.

July 9

We are trying to put away boxes and barrels.

The goat that has been loaned to us is acting sick. The Kaupena school children love to feed it, so they feed it beautiful flowers. That was so kind and thoughtful of them. One beautiful flower is called the Trumpet Lily. They wanted to do something nice for it. They did.

Sunday, July 10

We have no bread, so before going to church services I baked bread.

It is cold here at Kaupena with rain, rain, and rain. Larry didn't get back from the outstation services until around 2:00 p.m.

After _lotu_ church, one little boy came to our back door and cried, "_Kangi, Kangi!_" at least that is what it sounded like. At first, we couldn't understand what he was trying to say. Larry went outside, and in their excitement, several little boys directed him over the hill toward the goat house. Larry thought the word _Kangi_ meant animal, so he followed them.

"_Meme meme_" goat-goat is about dead. Its head droops. It hardly makes a sound, and it can barely stand. Its eyes are half open, and it goes "blaaaah-blaaaah." It is the borrowed goat from another missionary from another mission group, and we do not want anything to happen to it, especially on our watch, so we prayed for it. That was all we knew to do.

The Goat Lives!

Monday, July 11

This morning Larry walked down to the goat house to see how meme-meme was doing. It was standing and eating like a normal goat. One of the nationals told us the Trumpet Lilies have opium in them, and it masks an LSD trip. The beautiful flower given to the goat caused her to go **long-long**, loony or crazy.

Beautiful things may have our attention for a while, but after the flower has been eaten, it can cause havoc even death.

Thank the Lord, Jehovah Jireh—THE GOAT LIVES, with another ram in the thickets.

Damu the Witch Doctor

Damu, the witch doctor is old and looks like an ancient beachcomber. He is a short, barefooted fellow who always wears the same old soiled shirt, which used to be white. He wears dirty-white flimsy, surf island trousers. He too likes our goat. He comes, gets it, and leads it around. He also likes to stay around our house.

One evening, I found Damu sitting on our back door step waiting for me to come home. He couldn't speak English, so he pointed to his bare feet to let me know his feet hurt and they were cracked. He wanted to know if I had any medicine for them. I went inside and got some salve for him to rub on them. Did it help? He hasn't come back for more.

I don't hear anything about him practicing his craft now. He must be a retired witch doctor who comes to the missionary for medicine. We really like Damu.

We have no lawn mowers here, except for sheer muscle energy. There is a deaf young man who uses a bush knife (machete) to mow our lawn. He cuts grass, climbs trees to cut off limbs, and helps around the station. This is his way of earning *Kenas* money.

Lice

Children have little or no prejudices and they assimilate quickly. They mimic their environment; Mendy and the little national girls are prime examples.

The Papua New Guinea women tie their *bilums*, or string bags on top of their heads. It serves as a cradle for their babies as they lie in their string bag bassinet, or it can also serve as a type of an American woman's pocket book, or it has been described to be the man's truck for hauling loads.

Mendy and the other girls play with their *bilums* tied on their heads carrying a baby doll inside. Day by day they play, and one day I noticed at the nape of Mendy's hair in the back, were little white somethings. I had never encountered lice before and didn't know what they looked like, but I was quite certain what I was looking at were small white nits and lice eggs.

> One day I noticed at the nape of Mendy's hair in the back, were little white somethings.

Immediately, I washed Mendy's hair—daily and put vinegar on it. It takes time, but I attacked those nits with a vengeance. I separated her hair strand by strand and smashed each nit between my thumbnails as I went along—just like the little girls we saw when we first arrived in PNG. I learned lice eggs do not smash easily; they are hard, but we won the battle.

The best way I found to ward off unwanted predators like lice is to wash the hair frequently and use vinegar often, especially on the lice nits or eggs. You can even consume vinegar in moderation, and you don't have to be afraid of side effects, as long as you rinse your mouth after consuming it..

Vinegar and alcohol became my main defense for protection and cures. I learned this when I worked in the hospital in Frankfort, Indiana in the U.S. We rotated cleaning the utility room at night with vinegar and the next night with alcohol. Since then, I have used and proved its effectiveness over and over with scabies, infections, and as prevention. Actually, when we did experiments in the nursing lab, alcohol was rated as one of the leading disinfectants. We didn't experiment with vinegar, but my personal experiments have proved to be as effective as alcohol—in its own way.

Little Hands Built a Foundation

July 13

In Mt. Hagen, we got several cases of supplies, bought a small wood cook stove, and a 2000-gallon water tank to catch rainwater from our roof as our water source. The tank was so big Larry had to use Pabarabuk's big Fuso truck to haul it.

He built foundational walls for the tank to set on, but the foundation had to be built up with stones on the inside to make it solid.

Toward the end of the school day, I looked out the kitchen window and saw a line of young children coming single file up the mountain from the creek. I noticed each child had a hand size stone in one or both hands. I went to the bathroom window and watched as each of them filed by the wooden foundation and dropped their small rock into the large vacant area.

The rocks seemed to magically multiply. In a short period of time the rocks rose to the top of the foundation boards. The children's hands with their little contributions meant we could now have water on a firm foundation. One, two, or three rocks from the hand or hands of each young school child made a "mountain out of a molehill."

Again, God provided by the little hands of these precious children.

Malaria Madness

July 22

This evening we had tea at the Blackwells at Beechwood, an Australian Mission Camp down the mountain. This is where we learned we Americans scoop our food with our forks, as a German descent informed us. The proper way, he said, was to take your butter knife and push it up on the backside of your fork, and then place it into your mouth. I should try that; it may help with weight loss. They are possibly right; we are probably scoopers.

We had a nice time. It was the first time that I encountered Germany vs. America.

Mendy began acting sick. I felt her head and skin, she had *skinhat* an elevated temperature, so I asked Larry to take us home. I always feel uneasy when my girls get sick. I try not to, but it must be a fear of losing them that looms over me. I know I am to have faith, but it's a workout now.

Back at our house, we had prayer with her and shortly, she rose right up on her bed, got up, and slept well all night.

Saturday

Mendy is tired and listless with a fever.

Sunday

Mendy still has a temperature and has the "lazies."

Tuesday

Mendy can't seem to get into her studies. She gets very tired at about 10:00 a.m. each day with a fever, and then she goes to sleep. I'm concerned.

None of the routines I usually do for sickness helps her. **I am uneasy.**

Thursday morning – Larry took Beverly and Robin to Kujup Nazarene Hospital to stay with a missionary friend for a couple of days. I stayed home with Mendy. She is very sick. It attacks her between 9:00 a.m. to 1:00 p.m.

She's asleep now, and her axillary temperature is 102° and climbing.

Mrs. Smith, a European aid in PNG school affairs came to this area, and she stopped at our house. After hearing, and seeing Mendy, she said, "Malaria works that way."

She was a gift of information.

Why hadn't I thought of that, or had I blocked it from my mind? I started Mendy on Camoquin, the drug given to children with Malaria.

I sure feel restless with her so sick.

July 29

Larry was on his way back to the station from Kujup when a police car passed him. A rock flew up and broke the new station truck's windshield. It didn't have a screen shield to protect the windshield. Many vehicles have broken windshields due to so many stones in the road that fly up.

We rallied the mission's old rickety Land Cruiser to take Mendy back over that same stony road, beyond Mt. Hagen to the Kujup Nazarene Hospital to the doctor.

The doctor said he thinks Mendy has Malaria possibly with another unidentified health problem. He said, "If her fever goes up again, take her and have her blood tested while it is up."

Yes, right, just like that. How possible is that? We live in the bush with hours of drive time over and through potholes to get to the hospital, and if her temp spikes at night, and we get out on the road, worse things than a temperature could happen. It is unsafe to travel at night and sometimes even in the daytime.

Robin came with us. We overnighted in Mount Hagen on our way back from the hospital.

Saturday Morning the 30th

The girls and I are up, but we decided to stay at Mapangs, while Larry goes to buy station supplies.

Mendy went back to sleep early this morning. I went to the bedroom to pray after reading in the Bible where Jesus rebuked the fever of Peter's mother-in-law, and the fever left her. The healed woman got up and attended to those around her. It doesn't tell if she did or did not ever have a fever after that.

While I was praying, Mendy woke up and asked, "Where's Mom?"

She got up and started drinking liquids. She was well enough to go over into town. There was no noticeable fever. We even stopped at the city market and got vegetables.

Back at Kaupena: Mendy is sick again. She went straight to bed and is complaining of severe stomach pains. She is screaming, crying, and vomiting. It is terrible. I have prayed and prayed and I am ready to take her back to Kujup even in the pounding tropical rain, over the slick and dangerous roads in the old rickety truck, even tonight. Larry thinks it is too dangerous and too much of a risk to take for all of us.

Back at Kaupena: Mendy is sick again.

I have done all I know to do. I suffer too when my children are sick.

I went to the office, a little room surrounded by windows at the back of the house, where Larry was working. I was at my wit's end and with a grieving heart I said to him, "It's in your hands. I have done all I know to do."

A heavy dark cloud hung over our house inside and out. I left the decisions in his **h**ands, because I was not handling this situation well. She was so sick.

Larry walked into Mendy's room where she lay on the bottom bunk, and said, "We'll pray with her."

Larry prayed. I tried. She quieted down, and then we tiptoed out of the room. The slightest movement or noise distressed her. The evening got dark and turned into forever, or so it seemed.

Larry and I lay fully dressed on our two wooden couches. He lay on the one loaned to us, and I lay on ours. We waited silently, moment by moment through the long night for what may happen next. It was a l-o-n-g night.

Sunday July 31

Daylight broke and Mendy had slept calmly all through the night. Praise The Lord! Thank God for His mercy.

Larry told her, "If you drink a tablespoon of broth, I will give you a Kina." A Kina is PNG's dollar. It is a big round silver coin with a hole in the middle. She tried, but she wasn't ready to sip broth yet.

In the afternoon, I told her, "If you drink liquids, I will get you that pair of white platform sandals you saw and loved, which is in the Mount Hagen store." That sparked her weak attention. She tried hard to sip the broth, resting in between. Minutes turned into hours, and she finally drank the broth. She got her Kina and her shoes.

As I write this book, it has been over four decades, and she has never had another episode of Malaria to this day. Jehovah Jireh—God placed one more ram in the thickets. Praise His Name. He truly is our Great Physician.

It's Like a Stagecoach Stopover

August 1

It is August now in Papua New Guinea; the weather changes very little. It was much warmer at Pabarabuk than here at Kaupena. The Kaupena Station is just off the one and only highway going up through the Highlands. We are at the end of a little winding, dirt road that goes up the side of a mountain, when a landslide doesn't block it. The road onto the station is like the days of yore, dusty, and bumpy, and it comes complete with potholes.

It is somewhat like the old-time stagecoach stopovers, which come with meals, beds, and rest for the weary. Needless to say, it keeps the wood stove burning in between mission duties and teaching our girls.

The elevation is higher here than Pabarabuk; it saps physical strength quicker, and it takes food longer to cook. There are no microwaves for quick fixes.

Sometimes Australian and New Zealander athletes come to these mountains to train to enhance their physical fitness. For us, we just go to bed.

Chicken Meat

August 16

Chicken meat is relished the world over, at least in most places. Larry had our chickens moved in the daytime from across the airstrip to our side of the station…a human mistake. The next day, we noticed two of our chickens were missing. This is one thing the PNG people have in common with the rest of the world; they love to eat chicken, especially when it is free. It tastes much better—or bitter.

Graveyard Beliefs

August 18

Poki, a national, died today. He came in on stretchers about one and a half weeks ago. He had cancer and we sent him on to Mendi Hospital farther up into the Highlands. People are wailing. People came and wanted *dwai* wood for a *box* casket.

Steve Haynes, a friend of ours with another mission, and Larry went to the *matmat* cemetery. The custom is that a woman is not to go *to the matmat*. The people said, "This is something that belongs to a man, this is a man thing."

Poki's grave fell in, and it is the national belief that when the ground breaks, it means someone will die. Also, they believe whoever is the first to go to the *matmat* is not to leave until everybody leaves or else one of their family will die. Of course, we have no such customs and the missionaries got back in time for lunch.

Glaimi, a local government official's dad died this morning. They said he was old. When PNG folks in this area become *lapun* old folks, they stop eating and wait to die. This custom is acceptable in this culture. Larry is building another box.

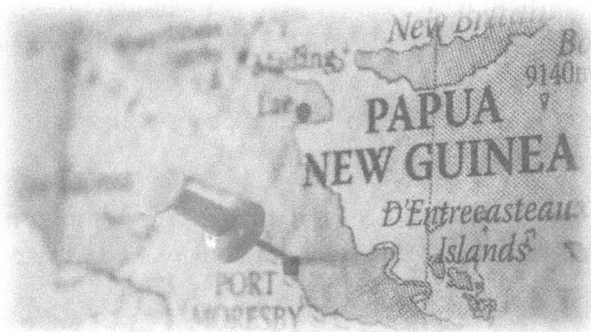

13: The Man with Twelve Wives

September 4

Larry went to the Tona Village today, up and over the mountain behind Kaupena Station. It was one of Togapa's tribal-lines and one of the last lines to stop their tribal fighting.

Larry said it was a hard two-hour walk. He said he climbed over tree roots, up and down mountains…and perspired. He said, "I was walking beside the river when my foot slipped and I fell in."

It makes me think of the children's song except with a little diversion, *"This is the way we go to church, go to church, go to church. This is the way we go to church so early in the morning*…sweaty, hot, and wet."

Larry said the headman of the village asked questions about salvation. He said, "I want to go to heaven, but I have a concern. I have twelve wives." He said, "They all fix me *kaukau* sweet potatoes to eat. My wives get angry with me because I can't eat all of their *kaukau*. When I can't eat all of their sweet potatoes they throw them at me. How can I go to heaven like this?" He voiced concern that these women with these problems would keep him out of heaven.

Larry said, "I told him, since you chose all of those *maries* wives, you are responsible for them. Make sure they have their own houses to live in and that all of your children are cared for. Then you go to your first wife and live with her. That is God's command. You are not to commit adultery or even lust after other women other than your first wife, the one with whom you were first joined together."

That is a hard truth when it is a new thought, even if it is an old thought, and not socially practiced. It really is not a new truth. It is as old as God's commandments.

The headman had a serious problem that he created by making wrong choices. Somewhere I read, you can't "unring" a bell. Wrong choices are hard to unweave, and sometimes they are so tangled that only God can make lemonade from lemons.

Peace

September 13

It is wonderful to have time to pray and read the Bible. I can't get enough of Christ's Presence. It is an out-of-this-world experience. I'm so unworthy. God knows what is best for me. The joy of the Lord is my strength, Nehemiah 8:10. The Lord's Presence makes such a difference in my life. It is also better for those around me.

September 14

This was a hard day from the beginning. While in prayer, it became very clear to me when ALL is against me, will I still stand and fight and not give in? Then I knew I must stand strong.

Larry went back to Imi Village to work on building a church, and Mendy finished first grade. I'm so glad for the space, or is it peace?

September 21

Larry went to Pabarabuk and borrowed their big truck to go to the other side of Mt. Hagen to get wet sand for concrete to build the foundation for a village church. On the way back, coming down a steep mountain the steel brakes inside the brake drums overheated the rims, and that made the rubber tires get hot. He got a toolbox, which was the only vessel he had, and carried water from a spring in the mountain to douse the rims. He said he was glad to get back to the station.

A fifteen or sixteen-year-old girl was carried to Beverly's house on a stretcher. She was having a difficult labor. We observed her from 12 noon to 5:00 p.m. The baby's head was in position, but her labor went into inertia, where the muscles were too weak to contract. Beverly got a truck driver and took the girl to Illiabu Sub-health Clinic.

Bev said the place needed housekeeping help. She left the girl there to be treated with PNG socialized medicine and by the medical staff.

We haven't heard from her since that time.

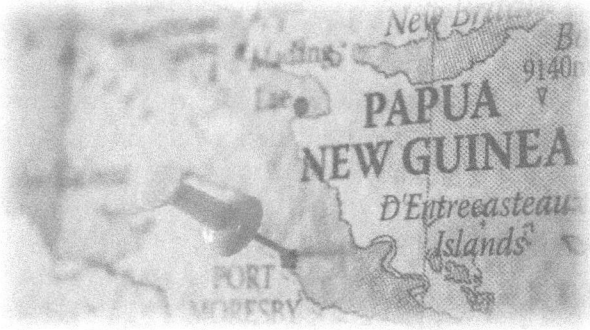

14: Medicine Bottles on the Bed

October 2

Our family visited the Rich family at the Mele Mission Station farther up into the Highlands. After our Sunday dinner, we were doing dishes, and I saw little Jenny Rich in the guest bedroom where we had been sleeping. I immediately went in and saw a bottle of antimalarial and anti-acid pills poured out onto the bed. The bottles were empty.

Of course, we became alarmed. Beulah, Jenny's mother, gave her mustard and milk to drink hoping it would act as an emetic. It didn't. Beulah tried to make her vomit by putting her finger down her throat. Nothing. She fed her a raw egg; still nothing. Sweet little Jenny liked to eat, and she seemed to actually enjoy the nauseous foods.

Mele is far back into the bush, so there was no hope of getting her to the doctor any time soon, for there is not a hospital anywhere near this area. Like so many helpless times, we turned to our Great Physician, the One who knows all, sees all, and loves all.

We gathered in the living room in front of the new river-stone fireplace, where the stones were popping and cracking. Once again we all got down on our knees asking God to intercede for this child in a desperate situation.

We sat, waited, and watched. Time went by and we saw no symptoms of distress...just normal, sweet, tough little Jenny.

Later in the evening: It was time for the Gray family to return over the dirt and stony roads back to Kaupena. We arrived back at our home station safe and sound. Jim and Beulah came up on our short-wave radio and said Jenny was doing fine.

We give another praise for our Great Physician, Father God.

The Burglar's Wet Feet

We arrived back home at the Kaupena station at 5:00 p.m. Beverly had a delicious hot meal casserole waiting for us. I made a double batch of biscuits, and we ate dinner at about 6:45 p.m., fifteen minutes after dusk. Quickly, we washed the dishes and then set out through the rain with our umbrellas to attend Lotu Church at 7:30 p.m.

After *Lotu*, I sat talking to some of the people from the outer villages when I heard the Head Pastor say, "Brother Gray is calling for you."

I sensed something unusual, so Robin and I followed the Pastor. She got to our house ahead of me. She called, "Mom come quick!"

It is not uncommon for the family to want me to hurry and get there... wherever. She ran out to meet me and said, "Someone broke the window and broke into our house!"

Larry had unlocked our front door, walked through the house, and unlocked the other locked doors. He noticed the office door was standing open. That door is always locked except when we are inside the office and sometimes even then. As I stepped inside the door, Larry asked me if I had the store money that the storekeeper brought just before we left for church.

The station oversees a store for the people and it also provides money for operating the mission.

I said, "I was in a hurry so I dropped the money behind the dresser in the girls' room."

"That's a relief."

The station money was still there.

Robin hurried into the office and noticed the curtain pulled out from the window and the air coming through. She remembered distinctly closing the window before she left for church. She started investigating further like Miss Sherlock Holmes.

The top of the office desk is level with the louvered windows. We pull the heavy curtains together at night while working there. It was that window in front of the desk that someone broke and came through leaving their wide, wet footprints with large tacky toe prints still on the desktop glass.

The top and bottom of the office desk drawers were open on the right side and the bottom drawer on the left side. The middle drawer on the right side is where we keep the station money until we go to Mt. Hagen; it was shut tight. The money was still in that drawer.

Thank the Lord. Jehovah Jireh. God does not sleep. He keeps a watch over His own.

The week before, Larry had preached an inspiring message, "The love of money is the root of all evil." After that, one of the government teachers paid her tithe. She had wrapped the money in a piece of plain yellow paper. Larry had laid it on top of the desk. We found it among the unanswered letters that had been dumped out of their neat little box by someone in search of money. There laid the tithe money while the "steal man" walked over the top of it.

After our investigation, we concluded the angel of the Lord had protected what money the mission had. Bless the Lord, Jehovah Jireh again and again…Sweet Jesus! God provided another ram in the thicket.

We concluded the angel of the Lord had protected what money the mission had.

Later, a report came that the man who killed Togapa thought he had killed Mark, one of our Christian government teachers. Now emotional turmoil is running high through the tribes, and Mark is concerned for his life. He came to live inside the fence next to our house.

He said, "I have a feeling that someone is around watching me." He said he felt this again this evening so much so that when the Head Pastor went to his door to get him to come to our house, he called out in fear, "Who is it?"

After Mark saw our broken window from the break-in, he became even more frightened. We invited him to stay with us for the remainder of the night. Since Beverly lives alone, we thought it would be good if Robin would go and spend the night with her.

About the time we all were settling down, Larry walked into the office once again to look at the crime scene. The light came…"The box. The gray metal box, where is it?"

He alerted me, and we both looked the house over. Nowhere, it was nowhere to be found. We looked at each other. Our much-guarded passports and visas, our income tax papers, Robin's school correspondence certificates, and our American checkbook were in that gray metal box. The thief thought he was getting a metal box of money, only to find out later that it was our very important papers, which meant nothing to him/her or whoever.

Stolen Passports

October 3

Early this Monday morning: I heard a key rattle and the front door shut. I got up from bed to face what this new day would bring. I heard Larry talking to someone at the back of the house. He came and told me that Mark had gotten up to go look for our stolen treasures, only to find a pair of Larry's shoes hidden under our outside building. Could the shoes possibly not fit or were too long? Larry is 6'2" tall and most PNG men are quite short.

Later in the day: I needed two _toea_. I asked, "Robin, do you have two toea I can borrow?" Two toea is like 2 cents in American money.

She told me, "Look in my brown purse on the desk in my bedroom." I looked and looked, and then became suspicious. She came in to help me look, but we decided her soft brown purse too had left through the jagged window. She was almost in tears. Her best friends' pictures, cherished letters, and ten American dollars she had been saving were in that purse.

Shall we repeat together, *"All things work together for good to those who love God, and are called according to His purpose."* Yes, we truly believe that. Perhaps God would use these items as He did the Ark of the Covenant as recorded in the Old Testament to trouble people's hearts when it got into undesignated hands and caused them to return the ark-stolen goods.

The ark of the covenant of the Lord was taken from the Hebrew people, the Israelites. The Philistines stole the ark and set it beside their Dagon idol god. During the night, Dagon fell to the ground on its face before the ark of the Lord. The men, who believed in it, took it and set it upright in its place again.

When the men got up the next day, they found their god had not only fallen but its head and the palms of its hands broken off, only the stump of Dagon was left intact.

The Philistine's solution was to get rid of the ark. It didn't seem to occur to them that they needed to get rid of the idol. God's hand was heavy on the enemies of Israel. The Philistines had stolen from God's coveted people that which didn't belong to them. To keep them all from perishing like their god Dagon they sent the ark to Ekron. After the Philistines sent it away, the Lord punished the young and old men of the city with a horrible case of hemorrhoids.

The Ekrons didn't want the ark. They were afraid their city would be fatally destroyed. The men who didn't die were struck with hemorrhoids. Their sorrowful cry went all the way up to heaven.

You can read the whole account in I Samuel Chapter five, in the King James Version of the Bible.

We pray that wherever and whoever this person or persons were that took the purse, God knows, they will become so convicted of their sin that they will give themselves up to God.

Larry went to Ialibu to report the event. Now we are waiting on the papers to fill out from the American Embassy in Port Moresby to replace our stolen passports.

A few months after the break-in, Robin went down to Beechwood camp where both missionaries and national women met for a get-together. She came home telling me, "I saw my pocket book, but I didn't make a scene."

October 5

Word got around about the break-in at our house. A national **schoolteacher** felt sorry for us and said, "I have a good watch dog you can borrow."

Now Jenny is with us. She is big, black, and looks like a German shepherd. We have to eventually give her back, but we got one of her puppies. We named the little fur ball Candy.

Melinda and her dog Candy

Later, after Candy had grown, she had a puppy and we named her Lollie, a Pidgin word for Candy. Pidgin is the trade language used by people over much of the island.

Halloween in a Third-World Country

October 31

The Blackwells had a Halloween party at the Australian Mission Camp down the mountain. The girls did our American custom of dressing up for Halloween. Robin decorated herself in different colored paints, and Mendy dressed like an Indian on the warpath. The girls strutted across the airstrip, before the unbelieving nationals of Papua New Guinea, in their American Halloween make-up. As they went across the airstrip, it hit me like a bolt of lightning. This is what the nationals do in their heathen practices when they sacrifice or make rituals for idols. Even though it was kid play to our way of thinking, it was real to the nationals; the way into their spirit world. It was as if I had insight into their spirit world of evil, and I wanted no part of it. Never again did I dress my girls up for Halloween or even celebrate it.

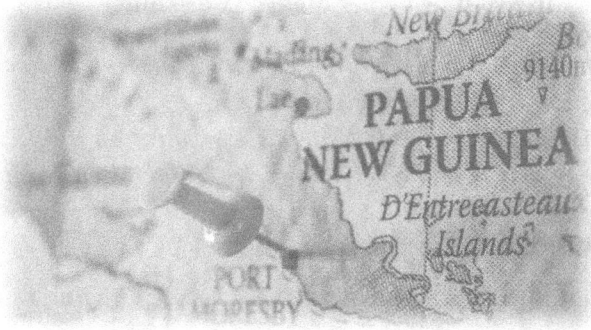

15: Unlearned Taught the Teacher

November 16

Larry and I, along with some of the station workers, went down to the *road bung* market to buy kumu greens and *kaukau* sweet potatoes, and plantain bananas to cook for the big "Christmas bung."

After we got back, I had school with Mendy until 12:15 p.m. and then dinner at 1:00 p.m. Lepi, our house help came and said, "The ladies are waiting under the tree for cooking class."

I get embarrassed thinking about this, but I went to PNG to teach the ladies, so I started a cooking school. I began the class with how to cook rice, something they had been doing for years. You know how we Americans can do anything.

What we do is by God's grace.

I showed the ladies step by step how to get the water hot and then pour the white rice into the big four-gallon pot of boiling water.

I continued teaching my wisdom on cooking. The class was almost finished and so was the rice.

I put my big spoon in and out came these gooey, sticky, clumps of rice.

I couldn't understand their language, so I don't know what they said about *Ambo kondoli's* rice or her dignified teaching.

> *After I had been around for a while, and watching them cook, I noticed their rice always turns out perfect—light and fluffy. I learned they put their rice into cold water as they put it on the fire. I still, to this day, cannot cook a good pan of rice like the PNG ladies do.*

The next cooking class is scheduled for next week.

One week later, I went back under that tree with material to teach them about *mun sik* menstruation, *meri i gat bel*, pregnancy, *mari i karim pikinini*, labor, and delivery. Yes, there was medical knowledge they received from me, but what I learned from them, about breastfeeding, became valuable to me.

Oh yes, I gave them medical knowledge about womanhood, but they had been getting pregnant since the first people on the Island. Menstruation they had no choice in. It comes every month, twelve times a year. For labor and delivery, they had their own method. They go to the river to have their babies. Again, once they were pregnant, they had no choice but to deliver their offspring.

What could I tell them about breastfeeding? My American way was not successful.

Oh, we Americans have it all figured out…don't we?

Holidays far away from home

Thanksgiving is a USA holiday where families get together. Here in PNG they come and go without our extended family. I get sentimental about this time of year. I am very family-oriented, but being away from family and friends is part of being a missionary and following God's call to go out to tell the world that Jesus is the light of the world. The Lord sees us and knows where we are and why we are here.

While I was feeling a bit bluish and missing the season's celebrations back home, a windy storm blew through, and it caused the windows of our house to fog up like it does in the wintertime in North America. It gave me a feeling of "It's beginning to look a lot like Christmas."

The wind kept blowing and it blew so hard that I had the girls to get up against the walls for protection in case our delicate wooden house did blow down. It provided a few moments of relenting anticipation. Later, I looked out our foggy dining room window and saw our big pit-pit science building had blown down. It was old anyway--but still usable.

It was amazing how the wind and its effect chased away my blues.

"And we know that all things work together for good to them that love God, to them who are the called according to his purpose." Romans 8:28 King James Version of the Holy Bible

Our Science bush building after the wind

Watch out for Wadi

November 28

The man's name in this chapter was changed to protect the guilty.

Wadi is on the station again. This evening, Wadi, a *long-long*, mentally, physically, or spiritually impaired man was seen on the station. We are told that back in his village, he took his two-year-old child and banged her head on rocks. The report was: Wadi had torn up houses, threw an ax at two men, and was seen walking around in his undies.

Not all men here wear undies. Many have a towel hanging down in front of them. The towel hangs to about their knees from their five-inch tall, bark wrap-around belt. If the man has no towel, he will find long, wide leaves, which they call 'tanket' leaves that come from a tall plant in the bush. The sprawling leaves straddle the bark belt and hide the backside of man's anatomy...except when the wind blows.

The tribe bears the responsibility for each of its members.

Wadi's tribesmen follow him around in case there is an unhealthy situation. This is the custom, especially when someone may be exposed to injury. The tribe bears the responsibility for each of its members.

Today, Wadi walked up the mountain onto the mission station, and then he turned and ran toward our house and then toward our station's truck sitting out front. With his hands tied behind him, he jumped up into the air with both feet kicking behind him- three different times bending in the driver's door to the station's new gray Toyota truck.

Kicking in the station's truck door did not stop Wadi. He kept on walking with his hands bound, while his tribesman followed behind.

Later, when he saw Larry coming down from the garage, Wadi came running into our yard. Larry, not knowing what Wadi had done or was going to try, braced himself for an attack. Wadi ran and jumped sideways into Larry. Larry steadied himself with a thrust forward. Wadi's tribesmen then took hold of Wadi and held him.

Larry did what he would do in our culture. He called for the police to help with this challenged man before he continued his path of injury. The village men put Wadi in the back of the mission truck, and Larry drove them to the jail.

Larry said after Wadi got to jail and when they gave him a big *shoot* shot, he fell down on the floor before them.

Wadi told Larry, "I'll get you yet." We live daily under the protection of the precious blood of Jesus and Jehovah Jireh our protector.

We had not seen or knew of Wadi before. Of course, it wasn't us Wadi was in battle with; it was the power of the enemies' darkness, trying to destroy the power of God's light.

Working with people of different races, with centuries of different traditional belief systems with their own defined culture is a time-sensitive situation.

The Threat of Death

It has been two days and Wadi is out of jail. Pondia, a tribal- line brother, brought him home – here at Kaupena.

I feel sorry for Wadi. He came over the hill led by his village brothers bringing him back from jail. They stopped at the Australian Beechwood station waiting on a Public Motor Vehicle PMV, but none would take him. They came to Larry, but Glaimi, a government minister, said, "I'll take him."

The girls and I stayed in the house with the doors locked. The word is out that he said he was going to kill Larry and those who took him to jail.

Delivered a Baby in a Ditch

December 10

A couple of men from the Tona Village, which is in the bush behind the Piamble Mission Station that is behind our Kaupena station, where they have no missionary. The men came to tell us the Village pastor's wife was in difficult labor, and they want someone to help them.

Larry told me, "You and Beverly can take the truck and go help her."

It was the first time I had been to Piamble. I didn't know where it was or what we could expect to find. We soon found out.

The road was a bumpy pasture field with barely a cow path. The first bridge, beyond the unoccupied mission house, was a typical bush road bridge, unstable and unsafe. Two big logs stretched from one side of the bank to the other side of the deep creek. The logs were too far apart for the truck wheels to cross over safely. Wangi, our faithful national chaperon, got off the truck, went into the bush, and gathered vines for ropes. He got down on the bridge and began to weave the vines in and around smaller logs on top of the big logs to rebuild and support the bridge before we endeavored to cross over.

A bridge in Papua New Guinea similar to the one we crossed; a Bridge too Far

Wangi finished tying the vines, and we began our passage…easy, easy does it. Little by little, I edged the tires onto the beginning of the logs on our side. With trepidation and a sigh of relief, I reached the other side where I was back on solid ground and earth. Those on the back of the truck, taking advantage of a free ride, had already gotten off— to save their life. After I crossed over, they climbed back to finish their ride.

The talk: "Two *ambo kondolis* white/red women have come to our village; one of them drove the truck…"

The pastor took us to the bush house where his wife was. Upon examination, it proved, sure enough; the baby was a footling breech with his two little feet ready to take off first.

The mother-to-be managed with help to get on the back of the truck and lay down. Her pastor husband and friends climbed on behind her.

Back over the same path we went with the lumps and bumps of the cow pasture—and the bridge. When we reached the vacant mission grounds, those on the back of the truck sang-out, "STOP, STOP!" They said the woman is in great pain and wants to get into a bush house to deliver her baby. I stopped the truck and planned to check her status of labor.

To our amazement, the mother-to-be jumped off the back of the truck and tried to get down the mountain to an old bush house; she only got as far as the side of the truck when she fell to her knees in the *baret* ditch.

Off in the distance, from the mountaintop, we could see rain coming toward us like gigantic sheer draperies suspended from the sky.

"Robin, go get the tarp out of the truck." She got it and spread it over us for a makeshift labor and delivery room, in the great outdoors, with dirt for the floor and a ditch for the delivery table.

Hidden beneath the tarp, the mother had a small amount of privacy… shielded from the curious.

This lady from Tona Village, a pastor's wife, and a victim of circumstances was blanketed with humiliation and shame; however, her condition was beyond her control.

There was not a doctor out here in "nowhere". It was up to two nurses to draw on their nursing resources, experiences, and God-given wisdom.

The mother's contractions began pushing out the fetus. Her only anesthesia was the numbing pressure against her cervical orifice. She didn't scream, but her muscles writhed in pain under the canopy of nature and at the mercy of the elements.

Then we saw two little feet pushing out through the cervix. We had to work fast. I literally pulled on the baby, feet first, with one hand as I held the other one on the mother's pubic area to fortify the fundus (uterus).

There he is! The mother delivered a precious baby boy, but for a few moments, there was no life and a zero Apgar rating.

We started baby CPR to resuscitate the lifeless little one. After a while, the baby gasped, and a heartbeat was detected.

Beverly quickly wrapped the newborn in a blanket and took it to the warmth of the cab of the truck to maintain its heat and to observe it. Robin stayed with me to hold up the tarp, while I worked with the mother's reluctant placenta.

After the mother was stabilized, she made her way to the truck where she could lay down in the back until we could get her and baby over to the Ialibu Clinic for a round of Penicillin, postpartum care for her, and neonatal care for "baby him".

When I got in the Toyota, the baby was pink and breathing. Beverly had worked until she got good circulation in the tiny little figure. We were hoping for a good hard cry, but for now, a whimper will have to do. At least he was alive.

The rain was upon us and we were still several miles from the clinic. We hurried the best we could over the stones, bumps, and potholes in the road.

I pulled into the dirt driveway of the clinic, and when I did, the truck dropped into a deep pothole and back out causing us to bump our heads on the top of the cab. The baby let out its first good hearty cry. Thank God for the hole, even though it may not have gone well with those on the back; it was good for the little one in the front.

We took the mother and baby inside the clinic. The *sisters* nurses took the pair on to a back room—beyond where we waited in the waiting room. Papua New Guinea has socialized medicine and Ialibu is not well supplied, so Bev left our bulb suction cannula with the baby to help remove mucus for a good patent airway. Both the mother and baby appeared to be doing well when we left.

It has been quite a day.

December 12, Monday

Sad! A national man came by today and told us the Tona baby died. Bev and I felt if somehow we could have brought the mother and baby here to our station, just maybe he could still be alive, but the American mission master and the Southern Highlands medical counsel, for some irreconcilable reason, closed our clinic, before I came to the station. The government clinic at Ialibu has limited resources.

Affix: Several years after we left PNG, a doctor from America went to Kaupena Station. He was able to get the mission clinic opened again. He has since left and returned to America. Times can get really tough in a third-world country…with limited socialized medicine.

The Return of Wadi

December 15

Moli, the station pastor's wife, came and helped me finish doing our washing. *Maybe someday I'll have the luxury of a wringer washer.*

Moli and I were in the house and we looked out the living room window and saw a man coming across the field onto the airstrip toward our house.

Moli said, "That's Wadi!"

Mendy was playing near the school, beside the road, where Wadi was coming onto the station. I sent Robin to get her…"and be careful!"

Moli and I watched him as he went toward where Larry was working up the way in the garage. He heard that Wadi was coming their way, and he went out to meet him. When Roli, Larry's garage helper, looked up and saw Wadi he said, "Where… can I go?"

Wadi walked up to Larry and said, "*Masta, mi gat bik sic.*" I have a big sick, meaning, "Would you pray for me and help me to become a Christian?"

We, in the house, watched Larry, Wadi, and Wangi go toward the church. Moli and I kneeled down beside the couch and remotely joined them in prayer.

Larry said later, "It was really easy to pray for Wadi."

Moli and I too felt that freedom and easiness as we knelt beside the couch in the house.

Later, Wadi came to the house, and we gave him something to eat. Afterward, he went back to his village.

Christmas in the Jungles

This is the big day, the day of the mission sponsored Christmas dinner for the village pastors and families.

The men dug a big hole in the ground, put wood in it, and then put hand size stones on top. They call that cooking the stones.

When the stones are burning hot, they remove them with wooden tongs and layer the stones in between the food in the other hole lined with wide banana leaves. After they have all the food and hot rocks layered in the earth's second hole, they cover all the food with banana leaves, tree leaves, or whatever they have to seal off the heat and steam.

Today, they cooked 50 pounds of beef and chicken with the hot stones layered between *kaukau* sweet potatoes, meat, cabbage, and plantain bananas, along with *kumu* greens. If they had other food, it was added too.

The food cooks down in the earth for about two hours and then it is ready. When they remove the covering; you talk about a sweet-smelling aroma, especially if you hadn't eaten for a while. Wow! It was delicious!

This way of cooking they call a *mumu*. Yum-yum!

As I mentioned before, the clinic has been closed for a while—due to some kind of dispute in America, so we had dinner and food inside the clinic building. Papua New Guinea people do not like eating outside. They are sensitive about eating around other people who may not have or be a part of what they are doing. PNG people are givers and sharers. It's said over here that you can tell an American in town because they lick their ice cream cones while walking down the street.

There was not enough room inside the clinic for everyone, so they sat down behind the clinic building more or less out of sight. A few of the louvered windows were removed, and the food was served by passing it out the open window space. It reminded me of the older Dairy Queen in the States where you drove up, got out of the vehicle, and went to the window to order your ice cream, only the nationals did not have the luxury of luscious sweet ice cream.

The food on their plates looked like high rises – stacked. Before the folks left, they stocked their *bilums*. *A bilum is* a string bag that is made of yarn or bush fiber that the women roll on their legs into a type of string, which they call rope. The rope is then worked into its own peculiar weave that results in a string bag. They use them as their pocket book, their suitcase, or to carry around their special possessions when they leave their bush house. The women also tie their bags in front of their foreheads and let the string bag hang down their backs. Today, they use their bags for carrying food, to and from the Christmas dinner, which is where the two cultures met.

Before they left, they began putting the food into their string bags. I wondered *what are they doing?* Those were not the manners my mother taught my brothers and me in Ohio.

We were considered new missionaries, but this seemed so greedy to me. Here we were furnishing food, especially for them, and they were storing and stashing it away to take back to their village for other people.

It took months of culture differences before I could come to grips with other ways of thinking and lifestyles. I learned so much from the people I went to teach.

> *I can see it clearly now. After being in the states for several years, it is not unusual at a gathering for those who are finished eating to gather up food of their liking and take it home with them. Even cultures inside of a culture can change. It's called sharing. Actually, it is a kind of exchange of friendships.*

Also, in the states, I hear how different government officials govern concerning other people in foreign countries; I wonder how much they, like me, do not understand what nationals of other nations are really saying. In PNG, what they say is not always what they mean. They *tok bokis* meaning, talk in riddles, stories, or parables for you to figure out. It takes one born and raised in a culture to understand the idioms and hidden meanings of a birth language.

A Boy Dies, Pig Bel

This morning, the people brought a little boy's body to the mission station. Larry made a box. Those who have no *diwai* wood for a box are wrapped snugly inside a small blanket, similar to a cocoon, with only their face showing, otherwise he would have been wrapped in a simple blanket.

Fifteen days ago, it was Jacob, a little schoolboy who died. The people said he had *pig bel*; they told us it happens here after people have eaten pig meat. After months of observation and since no autopsy was done, my hypothesis is: when they have not had meat protein for a while, and then they get meat, which they really like to eat, their system is overwhelmed with the protein, then it is too much for their body to process.

I wonder if this is what happened to the Hebrew children in the wilderness when they were so hungry and didn't trust God to feed them. He told them, since you are determined and you don't believe me and trust me that I can provide you a table in the wilderness, I will give you what you are crying for. There were quails by the droves (or is it flocks) flying in. The people wasted no time grabbing them up like hungry dogs and ate them. They died.

I wonder if this was the overstimulation of protein, the same type of thing the Papua New Guineans called Pig Bel.

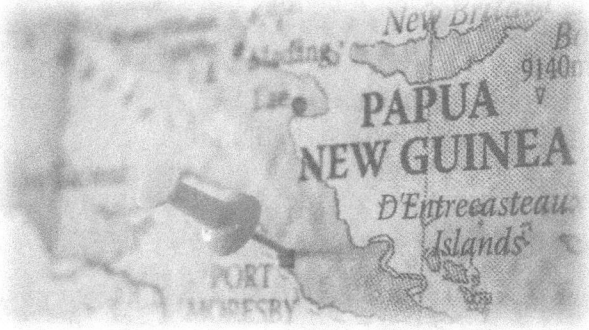

16: Bad News and Good News

February 7

Larry went to Mt. Hagen…mail time. We got word that my maternal Grandma Matthews died. Beverly received word over the *skid* radio that her dad died. Larry's mother wrote and said the water in Point Pleasant, West Virginia is contaminated. Mendy has a cold.

Feelings, feelings, and feelings, unpopular feelings at a time like this.

There is always room for a blessing; Robin finished her last home study math test.

The Man with a Truck Who Couldn't Drive

February in PNG

Papua New Guinea is a good place to raise coffee, which provides money for the nationals. The one thing on their mind is to get a vehicle. It is a real luxury to possess transportation in PNG. A moneyman, or men will sometimes pool their money and buy a vehicle even though they cannot drive. He or they will pay someone who does know how to drive to take him/them and the tribesmen around.

February is the month school begins in PNG. The school's summer months begin the last of November or early December.

Early one school morning in February, as the school children came onto the station, we heard a big commotion. Someone said a man had an accident. Fear paid us a visit…"the school kids!"…

"What about the school kids coming onto the station?" I asked with apprehension while getting to the scene of the accident.

The story went that the night before, some men had come to the station to stay all night with another friend who lived in the line-up of teacher's houses on the station. The driver was not in a hurry to get up and get out. However, the *papa* owner of the truck was anxious to get up and get going.

Whether or not the owner thought driving was a piece of cake, he went to try his hand at the wheel. He went out, got in the truck, and started it; when he did, the truck bolted forward. The owner pushed on the gas pedal instead of the brake. That sent him careening down the narrow driveway, which was partially lined with trees that ran along beside a ditch. He, in the truck, went off the right side of the road and crashed into a tree. He stopped…

He owned the truck, but he was no driver. He only thought he could drive it.

Thank God no child was hurt, even though they were all around.

Papua New Guinea Ladies

PNG has fine ladies in their tribes. They say they are grateful that missionaries came to Papua New Guinea. Jesus has set many of them free in their souls and minds. They are used to being compliant, which makes following Jesus easier than it is for the man who portrays that he is to always take the lead and do the instructing.

One young man declared, "Women are our trucks."

Women carry heavy cases of canned mackerel in their *bilums*, which hang from their heads. They even carry them up and down mountains as they

110

trek to their village. Yes, they do have neck and back pain. Yes, they do come to the clinic asking for something to help their suffering.

They are expected to take care of the pigs, tend to the gardens, and carry the food back from the garden, which may be a long way from their bush house, and they may be carrying a baby in the string bag on their backs.

We were told in the past the woman might even nurse the piglet if her milk was the only source of food for the pig.

The women are eager to learn, and as they learn, life for them brings a change, at least for the younger women.

I heard one young woman say that the girls are okay with the fellow paying a bride price for her; the more money that is paid for them, the better she feels about herself, as, "I am worth something." However, one woman told me in Sunday school class that she desired a new dress, but her man said, "I paid the bride price to your parents when we were married and that is enough."

Times change for everyone, even in countries such as Papua New Guinea, which was once known as the Stone Age. For some, pulling a pig around comes to a stop as they become educated. Today, women have businesses, drive cars, are airline stewardesses, and that progressive list goes on. One woman told me, "When the Bible came, it made a big difference for the women."

Ready

Here are the words I wrote in February, crying to God for help with something—I didn't know what.

Dear Father, I know you are well. You know all about me. You know every pain I have. If this is necessary to live with you, it will be worth it. Surely you see good in this. I don't. Father, you see a lonely heart right now. I have a fine family and precious children, but there are many things inside just bursting to be expressed. It is looking for an outlet. Father, you know You are the only outlet. I feel like I'm on the sea, tossing, fighting for something I know not what. Oh Father, please help me! Please!

This was the prayer I prayed in February, and I had no idea how God would answer, but He answered in a surprising way. I did sense that in six months something would take place. I had no clue what it was going to be.

Mendy's Prayer Worked

Mendy had prayed for a baby sister.

A few months later, I learned we were going to have our third child. I didn't understand. Here we are on the mission field where germs are like the sand of the sea, and furthermore, we are busy missionaries doing work for God.

I had forgotten that Mendy had prayed for us to have another baby.

My hormones always work overtime when I am pregnant. I get so sick. Larry took me to Mount Hagen to a doctor from England. He confirmed our suspicion. He also made light of the idea of going back to America to the White Castle Hospitals. He made another comment that stuck with us; he said, "I am here to make my mint and then I'm going back to England." We left him there in his office, never to see him again.

Larry got things ready to take me back to America. I was quite sick for weeks. I was too sick to sit up, and I couldn't even pack my own belongings.

Robin, in her own sweet way, consented to pack the bath essentials from the bathroom cabinet. She set a chair in the bathroom so I could sit and help make decisions on what to pack and what to leave. I sat for only a minute or two and then I had to go back to the couch and lie down. The other packers separated the things that were to be shipped back to America from the things to be left and distributed here on the station.

I said, "I am too sick to care about conserving space…just do it."

One item I left to be shipped back was a brown-handled knife that Mother and Dad had when they first went to housekeeping. It was a keepsake, but I have never seen it since. I also had to leave the package of chocolate chips that folks sent to us from America. I had kept them for a special occasion. Other items, memories, and precious friends we had to leave behind.

My nauseating sickness overwhelmed my care at that moment. Leaving America and going beyond to another world does not leave you the same person as when you left.

God is Calling

A missionary stood before a full congregation at a little country church in Ohio and told how natives allowed maggots to eat the dead flesh from tropical ulcers to promote healing. As a young girl, I sat spellbound listening, intrigued with his stories, but I never realized that one day I would be privileged to be one of God's called-out ones.

My Brother Ray on the horse-Brother Francis on the right-I'm in the middle.

I was about this age when I sat in Providence Baptist Church and heard the missionary tell about maggots.

Later, the missionary mentioned lipstick in another church, and the women giggled through their pink lips. That missionary moistened my desire for missions.

The first time I felt strongly of God's missionary call was in 1963. My husband, Robin, our eighteen-month-old, and I were living in Gallipolis, Ohio. We received a magazine in the mail at our address called *Mission Messenger*, but it had my mother-in-law's name on the labeled address. That's strange. It captivated my attention. On the front page was a picture of the Robert Harvey family; mother, dad, two brothers, and one sister en route on a commercial ship to Papua New Guinea as missionaries. My eyes were magnetized to that picture, as tears rolled down my cheeks. My body shook to an uncontrollable cry. An extreme happiness enveloped me. I didn't realize the Lord was confirming me. Each time I laid the magazine down, and when I went back to pick it up, that blessing of affirmation would flow all over me once more. This is the way "the call" began.

My husband wasn't a Christian at the time, so I pondered those blessings in my heart. One day he came in and said, "If you will move to West Virginia to my home place, I'll go to church with you." My eyes widened, and my heart pounded; *could this be?*

He got a U-Haul truck, packed us up, and moved us from Gallipolis, Ohio to way out into the country hills of West Virginia to a three-room blockhouse that he had helped his dad build when he was a boy.

He kept his word; he went to church—occasionally.

Christmas time came; time for a program. My husband consented to come to the young people's program. Toward the end, the youth group sang, *"Have you any room for Jesus?"* My husband held on to the back of the seat in front of him, and then he loosened his grip and fell at the altar of prayer.

Reluctantly, he yielded up his boyhood home and the hills he loved so well, to move from the country into the town of Point Pleasant, West Virginia, closer to church and his work.

The need for further schooling simmered in his heart. He groaned trying to do a home study course for lay speakers, but to no avail.

Soon the three of us, Larry, Robin, and myself were off to Frankfort, Indiana for Bible College. Our little burgundy Nash Rambler was packed, dragging a U-Haul trailer behind. Early the next morning, we pulled out leaving friends, family, and country behind. The farther we traveled, the farther from home we roamed.

Before we left, Robin, then three years old, had been sick and vomiting off and on many mornings. We took her to the Holzer Hospital clinic and the doctor checked her over. He first thought her blood sugar may be high, but the only thing he found was, maybe her blood sugar was a little too low. At daybreak, we started out with her lying down in the backseat...sick.

We moved on to Frankfort, Indiana headed to Frankfort Bible College. Robin wanted chocolate milk. Without hesitation that is what we gave her. From that day on, she had no more trouble with chronic sickness. Praise The Lord!

One missionary told us when we were talking about going to the mission field, "It's like stepping your feet out into the water not knowing what is beneath your feet or what is on the bottom of the water." They called that "faith." I still remember those words of wisdom many years later from Sister Lilly and Robert Harvey who have now graduated to heaven.

> After five months, the doctor detected something was not quite right. He could hear no heartbeat.

The Lord works in mysterious ways, His wonders to perform. Later, we learned we were going to be blessed with our second child. After five months, the doctor detected something was not quite right. He could hear no heartbeat. He put me in the hospital and gave me Pitocin to start my 'missed abortion' labor. (This was a spontaneous abortion, not of my choosing.)

I was admitted to the obstetrics floor, on the other end of the long, quiet hall, away from everyone. I was there from Wednesday to Saturday, and there was no labor. All of the wrestling with the uncertainties was overwhelming. The nurses were busy down on the other end of the hall where the main action took place. I cried alone and quietly.

Saturday morning the doctor came in and said, "It's a false pregnancy. You wanted to be pregnant so bad, you thought you were." That shot through me like a dagger. For one thing, I had a faithful body, and I had all the symptoms. In my heart, I knew he was wrong. I felt so alone and forsaken as tears streamed down my face. The staff did not share my grief. To them, it was in my mind, so grow up, and get over it.

I went home in postpartum depression. Nothing seemed right.

There was emptiness, depression, and desertion. What am I going to do? I had been collecting baby clothes, planning, and even wearing maternity clothes, and now…nothing? My recently purchased, old second-hand rocking chair sat empty.

The only thing I can do now is pick up my life and go on the best I can. Sunday, I went to Sunday school and then played my heavy accordion for the night service. By the time I got home, I wasn't feeling good. My stomach hurt. We had company, but I excused myself. The pain persisted throughout the night until I was on the bed, on the floor, anywhere to find relief, but relief didn't come. Finally, at about 2:00 a.m. my husband called the doctor, and he said, "Give her a couple of aspirins." My pains laughed at those aspirins.

I tossed, rolled, and agonized for another hour or more, and then to my shock, I gave birth to a baby, a lifeless baby girl. She had fingers, toes; so precious, so tiny. But, the doctor had told me, "You have no baby, only a false pregnancy." The doctor was wrong. Now, I look back on the incident and wonder, *what did he base his diagnosis on? He took no ultrasound. The only thing he did was use a stethoscope for detection. I wonder. I wonder.*

I had complications; the placenta wouldn't deliver. Again, Larry called the doctor, he said, "Bring her in." Shivering, cold, and bleeding, I held the baby supported in a bath towel. Larry threw my winter coat over my shoulders, and I made my way to the car. I felt the darkness of the night surrounding me.

The emergency room looked deserted, so they wheeled me up to the third floor. There was only one nurse and my doctor. They put me in the labor room, hastily cut off my flannel gown, and ordered a stand-by for blood. They worked fast and furious, concerned that I was losing too much blood.

Quickly, they wheeled me into the delivery room, still with only two attending people. The doctor said, "I'm going to do an emergency D & C" (dilatation and curettage). The nurse held the ether mask over my face, and I sank down into the deep.

As they wheeled me from the delivery room, and down the hall, my conscious spirit repeated from my unconscious state as the ether was wearing off, "Praise the Lord, Praise the Lord," I said again and again. "See I didn't lie to you, I didn't lie to you. I told the truth. Praise the Lord!"

It was in those next few days in the hospital that a new day dawned for me. It was as though I had been to heaven. My Father pities His children. He wrapped His love around me and allowed me to have His Spirit envelop me. I felt no depression and no loneliness. His light was mending my life together again. It was during those few days the inspiration came to me to work in the hospital.

When I went back for my post-obstetric check-up, the doctor tried to ease my burden by saying, "Nature has a way of ridding something we don't want." What he meant altogether and why he said it, I don't know and I didn't ask. But I would have asked... had it been today.

After recovery, I went back to the hospital, but this time it was to get a job. I was trained and hired as a nurse's aide. I had a robust curiosity to learn about medical knowledge. I went with the nurses and held the light for them. I couldn't get enough of learning. I learned to clean filth, and feces, empty bedpans, clean dentures, change beds and pamper patients. I loved being in the caring arena.

That exposure led me to the nursing school at Kokomo Indiana University, where I graduated in 1970, a few days after my husband graduated from Frankfort Bible College.

My husband had a U-Haul loaded with our stuff, ready to leave as soon as I got back from Indianapolis from taking my state boards to become a Registered Nurse. This was all part of God's plan preparing us for the mission field.

Larry stopped the U-Haul at Getaway, Ohio, about fifty miles from our "down the river" West Virginia home. Larry had been commissioned to pastor the Getaway United Methodist Church. While there, he enrolled in Marshall University to work on another degree, as I waited for our second viable baby girl.

We moved into an old, freshly painted, vacated house. The stories came. The owner's grandmother had lived there. One of her granddaughters was visiting when a big flood came. They had been reported to have walked down her yard, across the road to the high water bridge, and were never seen again.

An old building behind the house had a bell on the top; they rang the bell to alert the community for help. I was told, 'the bell never rang again.'

One warm summer night, from our raised bedroom window next to the bridge, there came a loud, hair-splitting, and eerie scream. It sounded like a woman. It came screeching throughout the air. We froze. We listened, "the woman!" After a few minutes, my husband said, "A cat."

One warm summer night, from our raised bedroom window next to the bridge, there came a loud, hair-splitting, and eerie scream.

One Sunday night about 9:15 p.m., Larry had dismissed church, and he stood at the back of the church shaking hands with the people. I felt labor was beginning, so I started for the house. I told Robin, now nine years old, to come with me. We walked in the dark, passed the graveyard, and over to our house where I waited a short while, and then I said, "You better go get your daddy."

I called the office nurse, she said, "Wait a while until the pains are regular." As a nurse, obstetrics was my favorite department, so I knew it was time to move out.

Our second beautiful little daughter, Melinda was born at 1:02 a.m.

Once again, eight months later, we packed up, and in my dad's old antique Ford truck, we moved to Boulevard Avenue in Huntington, West Virginia close to Ritter Park. We looked like duplicates of the Beverly Hillbillies without the oil. Stories of living at that place would make for another book.

It was at the Boulevard, late one night; Larry wrestled in prayer till the wee hours of morning. He had been reading *To Perish for Their Saving* about missionaries in Papua New Guinea. His divine direction was clear, "I want you to go."

Go we did, obeying God's call after being influenced by lipstick and maggots in the early years.

About the Author

Patrecia N. Gray (PNG) was born in West Virginia. She graduated from Indiana University with a nursing degree. She, her husband, and three daughters served as missionaries in Papua New Guinea (PNG) (for) over eight years. At the time of this writing, she resides in the country hills of West Virginia. A few of her accomplishments have been: Pastor's wife, Music Teacher, Registered Nurse, Health business, Missionary, Radio ministry, Writer and poet, Member of The Point Pleasant Writers Guild and West Virginia Writers

She had been published in the Guilds: Appalachian Heart, Recipes and Remembrances, ...Short Scary Stories, and School Days

She has been published in the Point Pleasant Register, Mission Messenger Periodical, the West Virginia Official Nurses Publication, and God Still Meets Needs—Littleton.

She is the author of three books at this time; *JESUS, Who is He?*, *The "Thing," mothman, devil, or spirits*, and *To Mother with Love.*

All of Patrecia's books can be found on Amazon.com.

Gray is working on several books waiting to come to full term to be delivered; including: *Memoirs of a Missionary Nurse II and III, Spirit of the Jungles; Jesus and Women; My Book of Poetry; and Little Patty Possible.*

www.ingramcontent.com/pod-product-compliance
Lightning Source LLC
LaVergne TN
LVHW051249080426
835513LV00016B/1819